Love, Hate, Fear, Anger
and the Other
Lively Emotions

Love, Hate, Fear, Anger and the Other Lively Emotions

JUNE CALLWOOD

NEWCASTLE PUBLISHING COMPANY, INC.

This book began as a series of articles in *Maclean's Magazine*. The writer wishes to express appreciation for the dazzling editing and direction from Ralph Allen, Blair Fraser, Ken Lefolii, Peter Gzowski and Robert Fullford. Thanks, too, to the staff of the University of Toronto Library for their patience and generosity in permitting me the use of their facilities.

Library of Congress Catalog Card Number 64—23219
Copyright © 1964 by June Callwood
All Rights Reserved
Printed in the United States of America

"Reprinted by arrangement with Doubleday & Co., Inc."

NEWCASTLE PUBLISHING COMPANY, INC.

EDITION 1971

ISBN 0—87877—002—

TO BILL

Contents

Who, Where, When, What and Possibly Why

Humans unfold into emotional maturity by a dazzling process of branching that no man understands. The history of man has been laced through with speculation, without developing a single incontestable theory about the origin of the emotions. This century especially, awed as no other by emotion's power to destroy life and sanity, brims with investigators so specialized that they are isolating themselves in foxholes of lingo.

If man could understand the black passions that make a fool of him, he would be better equipped to control them. The pursuit of happiness has become, in this age of ulcers and genocide, the pursuit of emotional health. It's a quest that finds the twentieth-century man, that genius with the rockets, atom smasher and pink deep-freezer, as baffled as the sweaty group in robes who assumed wise expressions when Socrates advised them to know themselves.

Some psychologists think we are closer to living compatibly with our emotions than ever before, thanks to the tickling of the brain with electricity, the manipulation of it with chemicals or a scalpel and the current personality preoccupation that results in mothers who term family squabbles "sibling rivalry" and athletes who solemnly analyze their death wish.

Many feel, however, that so much calculation and introspection is anti-living. Though the brain has been ransacked for its secrets, a million rats have scurried through mazes to illustrate the compulsiveness of drive and the questionnaire has invaded nurseries, no one yet knows how a man remembers his name, or why he laughs, or what will be his mood in a minute.

The search often focuses on the behavior of infants. Harvard's William James first noted that a baby's world was probably a "buzzing confusion" and that awareness of the universe must develop from the primary discomforts of hunger and cold. Babies are slower than puppies to notice their environment, anthropologists explain, because humans are still in the fetal stage for several months after their birth. They have left the uterus prematurely at nine months only because the female pelvis couldn't distend to deliver a more mature, and therefore larger, brain.

At first, the human infant lies in a vagueness of shapes, shades and meaningless sounds. He is aware only of being uncomfortable, and then of inexplicable comfort, a mysterious alteration which is the foundation of the sense of magic so acute in small children.

Gradually repetitions in his opaque existence print a thought, his first. His crying somehow provokes the more comfortable state. His subsequent purposeful crying marks the birth of reason, and the beginning of horror. The infant realizes that he is totally dependent and helpless, which gives rise to his first fear and his first anger. His first love, for his mother, is mostly gratitude; his first hate, also for his mother whenever she is tardy to serve him, is pure and murderous.

It has been a long time since psychologists believed that human babies come into the world already equipped with a satchel of elementary emotions. A fiery Johns Hopkins University professor, John B. Watson, was declaring vigorously in the 1920s that babies are born with three emotions, fear, anger and love. He deduced fear by their reaction to being dropped a short distance, anger by their behavior when he confined their limbs and love by their passivity when stroked. But other experimenters rapidly discovered that newborn babies are too dazed to care what a psychologist does to them and that later on (a) experts can't identify the emotion that causes the baby to wail unless they know what started it, and (b) some babies are indifferent to being dropped or confined but grow crotchety when stroked.

The emotional tone of a lifetime is established before a man learns to read. Some of it is constitutional: day-old babies have dispositions that vary from sluggish to jumpy. A physiologist's view is that these differences have been inherited. V. H. Mottram described the brain as full of spongeous gaps which messages of good or bad news must leap in order to arrive at the control center. The gaps aren't a constant width, even within the individual. They can be crossed more easily than usual, for instance, when the message is a familiar one or when the person is under the influence of a drug such as caffeine. The gaps stretch out when the person is tired or has been drinking alcohol. "In some people," declares Dr. Mottram in *The Physical Basis of Personality*, "the resistance [in these gaps] is permanently high and in others permanently low."

Psychologists won't concede that a man responds to moonlight according to the width of his brain gaps. Many of them are such extreme environmentalists, as opposed to hereditists, that they include the nine months of pregnancy as part of the factors that decide personality. Chemical alterations in the mother, as the result of profound fear, or anxiety, or long-term hatred and depression during the prenatal period, are believed to be the cause of some of the irritability, hypertension and colic seen in newborn babies. Observations of mothers and babies under wartime conditions in England offer convincing argument to support this contention.

Babies all seem to begin their lives, whatever the level of their pitch, in a state of undifferentiated excitement. After a relatively numb period while he recovers from the shock of his torment in the birth canal, the infant begins to sort out distress and delight, depending on his comfort. By six months, he is familiar with anger, hate and fear. When he is a year old, the process of observation and memory has given him an embryo sense of humor, moments of joy when he is played with, and affection—the beginning of love.

"The child's affections grow as he comes in contact with more people who are good to him," notes psychologist Justin Pikunas of the University of Detroit. "One important principle of the level of affection is that the baby must be loved in order to learn to love. Lack of affection causes a baby or child to withdraw into himself, too much affection, 'smothering,' may lead the child to become self-centered."

As the baby learns to separate people he likes, distinguishing adults from brothers and sisters, he simultaneously learns jealousy. He then begins to hate more enthusiastically and openly than he dared with his mother, whom he also likes very much.

In the second year, babies fluctuate between aggression, destructiveness, envy, sorrow, remorse and, more frequently than mothers will believe, contemplation. In the third year, the human miseries begin: inadequacy, guilt, anxiety, despair; along with them are pride, self-confidence, the ability to admire and a glimmer of individuality, which promptly causes stubbornness, contrariness and temper tantrums. A five-year-old has the same jumble of emotions as any adult and is beginning to master the grown-up technique of disguising them.

The greatest periods of emotionality in a normal lifetime occur during the mid-teens to the mid-twenties, when the individual finds himself overstocked with personalities, one to suit every occasion and none of them true. There is another rise of emotionality in the early forties, a steep rise between fifty and sixty, because despair over weakening influence leads to increasing sensitivity. Then there is calm until the flurry at the onset of extreme age.

The emotions of the elderly are heavy and hard to shake. Mainly old people are disposed to grief, self-pity, possessiveness, worry, testiness, boredom. They tend to be less responsive, even exasperating in their rigidity—in contrast with the fluid nature of a child's reactions. Psychologically mature old people are capable of benevolence, tolerance, sympathy, appreciation and satisfaction. Since the human begins in excitement, it is not unnatural that the very old end in passivity and apathy.

A meticulous psychologist, K. M. B. Bridges, noted in 1932 that children's emotions differ from adults' in that they are briefer, more frequent and lack shading. By adolescence the outbursts are being controlled, which means they submerge and become moods instead. The adult is so thickly larded over with attitudes and false faces that often he doesn't know himself what emotion he is experiencing.

Some personality traits seem to last from toothlessness to toothlessness. Among the most persistent are bossiness, conscientiousness, spunkiness, affection, nervousness and irritability. Dr. Pikunas has stated, "Later developments are to an increasing degree expanding and supplementary, rather than transforming, evolutionary rather than revolutionary."

Psychology is old enough to have some long-range behavior studies under its belt to illustrate this. A Fels Research Institute project launched in the 1930s recently reported on the personalities of adults who first had been observed as two-year-olds. One tot wept profusely when her mother tried to leave her in the nursery, at three was timid and tense, at six still very shy, at eight overly obedient and fearful. She grew up to be a meek, mild spinster living with her parents.

Another girl was self-sufficient and stubborn at three, competitive and demanding at five, later was always accompanied by an effacing, admiring friend. As an adult she shunned too close an association with men, enjoyed the role of adviser to weaker friends and trusted no one with her confidences.

Studies that span fifty years show similar results: whiners developed into adults who were chronically dissatisfied and pugnacious little boys became pugnacious big boys.

Fear is the emotion which seems to influence personality the most. A fearful child, one overexposed to strangeness, disappointment or protection, is off balance, requiring an exaggerated amount of assurance. His bloated need for love and self-confidence is impossible to satisfy, and consequently he is a difficult, angry and jealous person.

Love, however, is fear's opposite and provides both balm and backbone. Being loved, a small child's energies and intellect are released from the grind of protecting himself and conniving for advantage; his personality is warm, funny and curious. At a Philadelphia symposium on maturity in 1962, two University of Pennsylvania psychiatrists reported, "If the personal relations throughout childhood are good, then maturing proceeds adequately . . . If the personal relationships are poor, psychopathology of various kinds results. Psychopathology, apart from reactions to extreme current stress, is essentially the continuation of disordered patterns of human relations formed in childhood by improper treatment of the child."

"Hostility, violence and cruelty of all sorts are preventable by proper child-rearing," they added. "An effective beginning would be made if we devoted to the proper raising of our children emotionally a fraction of the time, money and energy we spend on raising corn, cattle and satellites."

The Scottish psychiatrist Ian D. Suttie commented, "Mental or nervous breakdown is merely the culmination of social strains which have existed since early childhood."

The luminous discovery of recent years, however, has been the ability of adults to dominate their own natures, despite the misshaping inflicted by a warped childhood. They set themselves in conflict with the perverse behavior and venom of their early experiences and somehow win through to steadiness, verve and decency. A foremost U.S. psychologist, Gordon W. Allport, calls this process "regeneration."

Those who accomplish their own regeneration must battle not only the effects of their harsh beginnings but also the tone of the society in which they live. Social class and history impose a personality ideal, which only the stalwart can resist. In the Middle Ages, psychoanalyst Erich Fromm points out, people were cautious, circumspect, unwilling to trust initiative. During the eighteenth and nineteenth centuries, swashbuckling adventure was admired; force and guile were considered virtues. Later the shopkeeper morality dominated, featuring thrift and orderliness. The present era is pervaded with what Dr. Fromm calls the "marketing orientation," resulting in troubled men and women who use charm, vigor and adjustment as competitive techniques.

Modern explanations of emotion cling close to the Latin root word *emovere*, which means inner turbulence. This avoids, as psychology has been careful to do for forty years, what is held to be the fallacy of separating emotion into brand names, such as fear, lover or anger. Such distinctions may be mirages, existing only in the eye of the beholder.

It's like trying to package a mist. Arrogance often masks insecurity, while humility is a disguise of arrogance. A man may be termed polite by one neighbor and spineless by another, calm by one set of standards and cold by another. The smiling depressives are among the most likely to commit suicide and maternal hatred commonly conceals itself under gushing embraces.

In an emergency, the muscles tense, the face pales, the mouth dries and the heartbeat thunders—all automatic preparations for either flight or fight. No man knows which he will choose until he has begun, nor is there a way to measure the element of cowardice in an act of public courage or the valor in a refusal to fight.

A psychoanalyst who addressed a famous conference on emotions, the Mooseheart Symposium at the University of Chicago in 1950, said he had never observed an emotion as a distinct entity, without nuances of other emotions, habits, sublimations, self-deception and inhibition. Love often encloses a grain of hatred because the lover has made himself vulnerable to hurt; fear has an edge of anger at the effrontery of danger and grief bears with it a considerable amount of self-interest.

Before psychologists became irresolute about labeling emotions, they used to believe that any sprightly explorer could chart human behavior. Descartes mapped six primary emotions: love, hate, astonishment, desire, joy and sorrow. Kant described five feelings: love, hope, modesty, joy and sorrow. William James said there were four: fear, grief, rage and love. Lint-pickers, before and since, have listed as many as five hundred.

A new method of surveying had to be established. What evolved was the theory that emotions are only sand dunes, so shiftable that they are unworthy of names. The problem is to understand the desert and the prevailing winds. Carl G. Jung made an important contribution when he established two divisions of personality, extrovert and introvert. The former he applied to those who sally out and grapple with reality, and the latter to those who peer at the world through distorting windows and avoid it. Everyone, however, is a combination of both systems.

Twenty years ago psychologist W. H. Sheldon divided people according to temperament-physique. Persons with broad trunks, short limbs and a tendency to middle-aged fat, he said, have comfort-loving, relaxed and social natures. Those who are lean, long-limbed, narrow-faced share a temperament marked by inhibition and aloof thoughtfulness. Athletic types, with well-proportioned bodies and good muscular development, are associated with vitality and push.

There is even a cheerless predictability as to which mental illness each type is disposed to develop. The chunky people, some experts believe, are cyclothymic, which means subject to fluctuating moods; the lanky people schizothymic, which denotes a tendency to withdraw from reality, and the athletes can be either.

Dr. Sheldon's grouping is a variation on the trait theory of behavior, in and out of favor since Hippocrates propounded *his* four temperaments—choleric, sanguine, melancholic and phlegmatic.

Whatever the classification, emotional behavior means irrational behavior to most people. The current ideal is that fear be mute, depression uncomplaining and anger nonexistent, which accounts for most of the dysfunction in hearts, stomachs and elimination systems. A man determined to ingratiate himself can legislate his personality so he never shows distress, but he'll blight his digestion, exhaust his heart and ulcerate his stomach.

This side of the grave, there's no such state as an absence of emotion. Controlled, unruffled people, in fact, often have a higher degree of measurable tension than volatile types. A University of California test discovered that teen-agers who were the least talkative, attention-seeking, animated and assertive, the most responsible, good-natured and co-operative, were also the most tense. They were bottling up tumult for the sake of popularity. The paradox of emotion is that weak personalities, those who are oversensitive, take criticism poorly, are arrogant and quick to anger—in short "emotional" by most definitions—have less emotional power than the mature, who tend to steadiness, reason and calm.

Epicurus and a billion thinkers since have believed that in the area of emotions there in wisdom in moderation. Mild emotions are pleasant, they observe, while wild ones are always disrupting. There is a body of laboratory experiments to support this theory. Earthworms, it has been noted, extend themselves luxuriously when stroked gently, but thicken and withdraw when the stroking is stronger. Fish swim toward a weak light and bend away sharply from a strong one. Scientists have often been thrown into confusion by lab animals who enjoy mild shocks meant to dissuade them.

Similarly, mild fear isn't distressing to humans, as witness the popularity of midways, ski jumps and speeding on highways. Extreme joy, however is both exhausting and physically painful. Apprehension is a boon to actors and athletes, stepping up their brains and muscles, but panic fills them with cement. An angry man is a formidable opponent, but a man in a rage is a fool.

The fallacy in the Epicurean philosophy is that will power cannot regulate emotions, but only can control the superficial display of them. A man becomes the master of his emotions only as he matures, by which time the knack is innate and he doesn't know how he manages it. Until then, men and women are near-helpless in the grip of their emotions, which don't fight fairly and can deal a death-wound.

Physiologists have learned that no emotion, once launched, ever disappears in the universe of the human body. Strong ones linger in the system, maybe for months. Cats, X-rayed some time after a barking dog had terrified them, still showed an internal state characteristic of fear. Leftover anger can make a man curse vilely because he can't find a comb, three days after a friend's insult.

Emotion has been producing the same startling changes within the human body ever since the Pliocene man. Fear, anger and hatred all cause the heart to step up its blood output as much as two-thirds. The liver releases a flood of sugar for energy, processes in the alimentary canal become erratic, adrenalin flashes through the veins to strengthen muscles and arouse the brain to a glittering pitch.

It was all very handy for dealing with carnivores in the swamp, but is most unsuitable when the same massive alert responds to a summons from a vice-president. The practice of capping interior chaos with an affable smile is a leading factor in heart disease, gastric ulcers and hypertension. Emotions, to be healthy, move out and are appropriate. Anger at an injustice is rather enjoyable, and so is hatred of tyrants. All the emotions associated with affection and interest are enormously beneficial. People feel exuberantly alive and efficient when they are learning or loving, but even a borderline state such as embarrassment results in physical discomfort and an impaired ability to think.

It may be that habitat influences personality, in that each person is a bouquet of possibilities and tends to put out those blooms which fit in best with the neighbors. Frenchmen, consequently, are encouraged when they feel libidinous by the knowledge that promiscuity is expected of them, while a New Englander with identical impulses is constrained by his heritage of austerity and self-denial. It is interesting that northerners in countries as disparate as China, Germany, Italy and Scotland generally show the same qualities of toughness, grit, vigor, frugality and quick speech, while southerners in those countries mainly are ingenuous, soft-spoken and languid.

Even weather has a notable effect on temperament. Researchers have observed that tempers rise in direct ratio to the fall of the barometer. On cloudy days people feel sad and cranky, while sunshine is a recognized therapy for depression.

Gender is also a factor in displays of emotion. Five-year-old girls are as demonstrative as five-year-old boys, but eventually the social pressure on boys to be "manly" calcifies their behavior so they rarely weep. Grown women show their emotions more than men do, which probably contributes to their longer life spans. Ortega y Gasset has written that the suppression of emotion is the greatest error of Western man since the Renaissance.

There is plenty of speculation about emotion, but no one yet knows what elements a human being puts together to produce a feeling. There are happy warriors all over the world who hack at the brain, searching in its ganglia for the mind —the god in the machine—as their forefathers fingered through entrails to locate the soul. The quest began nearly a hundred years ago when surgeons discovered that a certain area of the brain directly affected speech. At about the same time, a railway worker suffered an accident with a hot crowbar which cleanly removed the front part of his brain, leaving him alive but with a personality drastically altered to the bestial. Doctors eagerly inferred that the brain is chock full of control centers, one for every emotion.

Operations on the brains of cats subsequently established that there indeed is a lower brain full of hatred and rage. One anthropologist calls it the fossil brain, because of the likelihood that it is a living remnant of early man's brain, dominated for the past few thousand years by the development of another, thinking brain. The hypothalamus, thalamus, lymbic system and reticular formation, all knots of nuclei deep in the brain, are the seats of emotions.

The brain itself, three pounds of gray porridge, has about ten billion nerve cells or neurons. Two thousand million of them are in the hypothalamus; they are in all sorts of shapes and sizes, all of them zealously storing up grudges and shooting messages at one another by means of low-watt electricity.

When part of the brain is damaged or removed by surgery, an astonishing reserve system steps in smartly with its lines already learned. Memory seems to permeate the entire brain: dice a brain as tiny as you can and each speck will remember the lyrics to "Easter Parade," the pattern of wallpaper in a childhood bedroom and the route to the office. "Thought," wrote philosopher Henri Bergson admiringly, "is a dance of molecules in the brain."

Recently neuropsychologists have been making sophisticated experiments on living brains, directing mild electric charges into various regions. They have found that the brain, like many other parts of the anatomy, likes to be tickled. Certain "pleasure centers" have been discovered in cats, dogs, monkeys, apes and the bottle-nosed dolphin, an animal rated as intelligent as some men. The pleasure is sometimes so intense that the animals ignore their food, preferring the bliss of their electronic orgy.

When Dr. James Olds, then of McGill University, Montreal, outlined his experiments in brain stimulation before the 1955 Nebraska Symposium on Motivation, a psychologist demurred, "If we could feel all the rewards of eating without eating, would we eat? . . . Plugging itself into an Olds-intermittent-stimulation socket, what happens to civilization?"

Since the brain's electricity is chemically generated, another branch of personality manipulation has concentrated on chemicals. Currently, mankind has the doubtful blessings of drugs that produce euphoria, or passivity, or excitement. In the future, its advocates claim, the human personality will be produced by a precise prescription, obtainable at any drugstore.

It's not likely. No chemical or electronic thrill or scalpel has yet discovered what center of the cerebral cortex, the civilized brain, produces compassion or tact or good taste. England's great physiologist, Sir Charles Sherrington, studied brains until he was in his mid-nineties. He once observed, "I can find no explanation of the mind in terms of the brain."

The search for the mind hasn't been confined to needles, pills and knives. Ever since Freud, men have hoped that the blackness of the unconscious mind, where man hides every event and thought of his lifetime, would yield up an explanation of his emotions. Spelunking psychiatrists have probed for half a century, but the unconscious keeps its secrets. It was hoped for a time that the study of insects would be helpful, since they operate almost exclusively on instinct. The scientists ended with nothing, save an increased respect for insects.

The Russian conditioned reflex expert Pavlov spent twenty-five years collecting the saliva of dogs from their punctured cheeks and an Oxford zoologist has spent his adult life transfixed by the behavior of an earnest little fish called the red-bellied stickleback, but the mind remained elusive. Some experiments are bizarre in the extreme: in order to study aversion, women volunteers were requested to cut off the heads of live rats. Another such project used chimpanzees and watched their reactions to the decapitated head of another chimp. Other experiments are whimsical: psychologists once disguised themselves as trippers and accompanied a group of university students vacationing on the Isle of Man, making copious notes on their conversations and antics. In Florida, an enchanted scientist has succeeded in teaching a dolphin to whistle.

A recent trend in psychology is to translate emotions, instincts, passions and human nature into algebraic equations. One scientist proudly announced that he had succeeded in transposing into a mathematical equation Hamlet's feelings as he watched his uncle praying. Psychologists of this ilk never use such quaint words as anger, or courage, or loneliness; they substitute "need-satisfying," or "conditioned motor reflex," or "instrumental avoidance response." Laboratory clarity may be advanced minutely, but the science is in danger of detaching itself entirely from its subject: people.

It is consoling to find that every scientist who steps back from the workbench long enough to get a good look discovers that man is much more wonderful and complicated than he suspected. For one thing, humans have a natural flair for stability. Physically, they are loaded with safety devices: extra organs everywhere and overbuilt parts like a liver ten times as large as it needs to be. Emotionally, people can endure incredible stress and tragedy and still recover their former equilibrium.

"The living being is stable," wrote the French physiologist Charles Richet in 1900. "It must be so in order not to be destroyed, dissolved or disintegrated by the colossal forces, often adverse, which surround it."

There is even a natural proclivity for the emotions to mature, as there is for the body. Given even a modest diet of food and friendship, many people can sift through the falseness within themselves and arrive at their core personality, their essence and individuality. The matchless neurons of the brain bustle about, putting together cause and effect, working out rules of justice, calibrating the quality of wisdom and producing bloom.

It's an ideal in which lozenges of chemicals, joy-popping electrical impulses and bar-pressing mice seem totally alien. Man's mind remains his own. "In the latter stages of growth," writes Brandeis University's Abraham Maslow, "the person is essentially alone and can rely only on himself."

Love, Hate, Fear, Anger
and the Other
Lively Emotions

CHAPTER ONE

Love Takes Thirty Years to Learn

Love is the only emotion that isn't natural, the only one that has to be learned and the only one that matters. In recent years psychologists and psychiatrists have been making discoveries about love which tend to disprove three thousand years of poetry: real love is a skill rarely learned before the age of thirty-five. No love, not even maternal love, is instinctive or innate. Most people can love only in shabby, suspicious amounts; when they speak of love, they mean getting it, not giving it.

Yet the world never needed the knack of loving more than it does at this minute, if universal slaughter is to be averted. An Indian woman, speaking at a mental health conference in Paris in 1961, drew a standing ovation when she risked ridicule and urged that the world arm itself with the perfect love that casts out fear. "In the atom age," she said simply, "there is no other way whereby man can survive."

Many experts believe that love can be accomplished only

by people who have spent the first twenty years of their lives in a harmonious, loving family—a requirement that accounts for the observable scarcity of mature love in modern society. There is, however, a baffling proportion of adults who endured what should have been a blighting childhood but managed anyway to teach themselves how to love, by valiantly, stubbornly, patiently putting forth confidence instead of distrust, sympathy instead of skepticism and warmth instead of wariness. Rarely subjects of a psychologist's study or a psychiatrist's case history because they are well, the emotionally self-educated are among the most remarkable and heroic people on earth.

Examination of others damaged by love-deprivation in their early years is a sad business. Love has been found so vital for babies that a total absence of it will either kill them or reduce them to imbecility or madness. Doctors now seriously term love a nutrient and compare its role with iodine and vitamin C. There is some evidence that love even influences the growth of children's bones. It certainly affects a child's ability to learn in school; it is the foundation of emotional health, the magic wand that lifts the curse of self-dislike. Inability to love, wrote Dostoevsky, is the definition of hell.

Love has so many meanings that it can be used to describe different people's attitude toward God, sports cars, geraniums, the New York Mets, philosophy, individuals or the entire human race, stretchie socks, folk songs, solitude, the *Racing Form*, automatic dishwashers, babies, open fireplaces, the color pink and bird-watching. A pastor has found such variety in the meaning of love that for thirty years he preached every sermon on the same text: God is love. The word is even applied to weapons of death: Napoleon's soldiers grew fond of the cannons they hauled over the Alps, decorated them with flowers, kissed them soundly and gave them cloying names. In recent wars, men have found endearments for B-25s, Sherman tanks, minesweepers and bazookas.

Mangled as its definition may be, love is the most desired

commodity in the world, the only emotion whose existence can make life a personal triumph. In the past few decades, scientists have been concentrating tools of research and intuition on this sweet abstract, hoping to catch love as neatly as a migratory bird, band it so its life history can be traced and issue tracts on its care and feeding. The experts give the impression that they can't decide if they are dealing with a bird, a plane or Superman, but the sleuthing has been uncovering many aspects of genuine love that have never before been understood.

It has been observed, for instance, that people frequently look for love where it isn't—in shallow gregariousness, or in covetous parenthood, or facile romance, or sleep, food, new clothes, sex, alcohol, smoking and chewing gum, the last two regarded by the Freudians as adult versions of thumb-sucking. The most grotesque of the commercial exploitations of the universal need for love is a wind-up doll, a great success, which repeats "I love you . . . I love you . . . I love you" until its owner is sated.

It's not surprising that even preposterous forms of love are hard to refuse. A life without love, according to modern psychologists, is a life of destruction and insanity. They also have discovered that while anger, hate and guilt bloom in the bassinet, love, sympathy and tact require decades of steady tutelage.

Love, the scientists feel, is a personality's victory over unavoidable doubt and worry and carries traces of its spoils with it. Love begins in an infant who sensuously enjoys being fed and rages when hunger makes him feel uncomfortable. Gradually the baby becomes aware that his mother is the twin source of both his well-being and pain. The first efforts of human imagination are the hate fantasies the baby conceives against his mother and the longing for the better world of sleep and a full stomach.

Since his mother is his only safety, the destructive notions of punishing her are alarming. The baby is faced with the problem that will endure as long as he lives: how to handle mixed feelings. He can only practice on his mother or whoever tends him and obviously his success rests on the mysterious ingredient, his born-in-the-bone natural ability, and also on the balance of frustration and affection he encounters. An infant who experiences too much neglect is usually permanently embittered; too much mothering will stunt his development. The technique the baby evolves to cope with his cradle environment sets the lifetime tone of his personality. This period, the first three years but most crucially the span between six and eighteen months of age, is known as the critical period and corresponds to the critical period of plant growth, when it puts down tap roots and will be stunted if disturbed.

The presence of an attentive, affectionate and reliable mother, or mother-substitute, makes it possible for the easily angered and panicky infant to relax and believe in goodness. He gains confidence in his ability to master the dark, dangerous passions within him. His mother's continuing presence is proof that he isn't loathsome; in fact, it is constant testament to his value. The baby's natural curiosity is liberated from the vines of fearfulness and his intelligence can flourish. He becomes perky and good-humored. He is utterly charmed with himself, and charming.

In time, he emerges from the pure state of self-preoccupation that characterizes all babies and many infantile adults. He begins to care about his surroundings as separate from him and wonderful, rather than feeling he is Warty Bliggens, Don Marquis' memorable toad, who believed himself the center of a cosmos created expressly for his comfort. With his basic need for love adequately supplied, or nearly so, he can go cheerfully about the work of maturing.

In the beginning, he learns to love a pet or a toy, to make a friend, to respect property. Around the age of ten he can see his parents distinctly for the first time and love them. They are only tied, however, with buddies of the same sex, a few kind adults such as a teacher, a baseball coach or a sympathetic aunt, an idol or two.

Preadolescence is the most luxurious period in a lifetime for the growth of an ability to love. Unless the home is wildly unreasonable, the child lives in a plateau of friendships and has no inkling of the upheaval of lust ahead.

If the environment holds stable, adolescence launches a sex drive almost free of anxiety, desperation and gluttony. The teen-ager whose family has given him both affection and responsibility throughout his development is unlikely to equate promiscuity with potency, defiance or love.

By the time the young adult sorts out the hurly-burly of his twenties and arrives happily at knowledge of his real nature, he is capable of full-out mature love, acknowledged by the Quaker William Penn to be the hardest lesson in Christianity. Being able to love will bestow on him compassion, vitality, insight and courage, and he'll never lose them.

It's an ideal state rarely realized. Most people suffer battering along the way, which prevents them from ever loving without a limp. The earlier the injury—which invariably is caused by an absence of love—the more devastating the damage. There is even a strong likelihood that an angry and rejecting mother impresses her unborn baby with her dislike. Dr. Louis Gluck, professor of pediatrics at the Yale School of Medicine, said in 1962, "Studies show mother's state of mind during pregnancy has a great bearing on the child's early emotional behavior. If she has tensions and fears during pregnancy, she will probably have a fussy child with feeding problems."

The postwar years, when thousands of displaced children tragically were available for study, provided evidence of what psychiatrists had suspected: that humans put down foundations for loving in their infancy. If the early start is muffed, the personality may teeter everlastingly neurotic.

One famous study, headed by Dr. René Spitz, dealt with 239 children who had been institutionalized from their birth for a year or more, about half of them being cared for by their mothers in the institution and the rest by overworked personnel in the ratio of one nurse for every ten babies. The mothered babies had no fatalities and were progressing normally when the scientists examined them. In the other group, although nourishment was of a high standard and health precautions rigidly observed, 37 per cent of the babies had died. The only difference in their care had been that no one had time to croon to or cuddle the motherless babies. With one or two exceptions, Dr. Spitz found that survivors in the second group were "human wrecks who behaved either in the manner of agitated or apathetic idiots."

Dr. John Bowlby, who has taken a leading part in the study of love-deprivation sponsored by the World Health Organization, describes a four-month-old-baby seen after the infant had been two months in hospital. The child appeared to be dying. He weighed less than at birth and breathed so weakly that he seemed likely to give up the effort entirely at any moment. He was sent home and visited twenty-four hours later. The astounded doctors found him cooing and smiling and, though his diet was the same as he received in the hospital, he had gained weight.

Deprived babies are miniatures of adult melancholia. They don't smile, never respond to visitors, gain and grow very little in spite of healthful food, sleep badly, show no initiative, don't enjoy eating, seem unintelligent, are weirdly silent or cry endlessly. "Love hunger is a deficiency disease, exactly as is salt hunger," remarked Dr. Abraham Maslow of Brandeis University.

The effect on adults of early years in understaffed institutions or multiple foster homes has been studied frequently. The most severe cases are the psychopaths, people with such skimpy emotions that they are incapable of loving anyone or developing a conscience. Alarmingly, psychopathic mothers produce children exactly like themselves, their babies being as totally deprived of love as their mothers were.

But human beings have an infinite and joyful capacity to upset prediction tables and baffle the learned. A love-deprived background turns up whenever psychopaths are studied, but love-deprived backgrounds do not always produce psychopaths. Even among the psychically destroyed infants described by Dr. Spitz there were "one or two exceptions." A University of Chicago symposium on feelings and emotions in 1950 puzzled over two sisters whose father was the town drunkard and whose mother was insane. The girls were abused from birth and placed in several foster homes, one operated by a woman who later was found to be insane. Yet the girls calmly progressed through school at the normal rate, found good jobs and were proficient in them and married happily. Except for a few aches and pains, they were thoroughly sound.

"How did they do it? I don't know," commented Anne Roe, research psychologist with the U. S. Public Health Service, reporting on the sisters. "We still do not know how adjustment takes place beyond childhood levels."

Far more often, children who suffer love-deprivation for a considerable period during their early lives—up to the age of six, approximately—will show scars. Many of them spend their lives looking for substitute mothers. "Every relationship with another adult seeks to establish dependency and ask for comfort and assurance," wrote Dr. Bowlby. A Scottish psychiatrist, Dr. Ian D. Suttie, believed that adults tend to mold their environment to a shape that most resembles the mutual-caressing relationship of a blissful baby and mother. What they hope to attain is the radiant comfort of silken possessions, total power, uninterrupted praise; they seek the psychic stroking of love without end.

In such cases, there are excessive demands for the treats of childhood: food, money, clothes and privileges. Often this is accompanied, for the sake of being irresistible, with a bustling show of gaiety. Such people are easily depressed and, in Dr. Bowlby's words, "in constant danger of cracking."

Oddly, lack of love produces physical defects, the most startling of which is an impairment in bone growth. Dr. Griffith Binning, medical director of schools in Saskatchewan,

Canada, studied eight hundred school children and found that lack of affection caused "far more damage to growth than disease." Children raised in the horror of orphanages a generation ago were distinctly small for their ages.

The state of being loved, as internists know, is also good for digestion and circulation. Gastrointestinal disease, according to an investigation by the Chicago Institute for Psychoanalysis, is related to love-deficiency. And so, surprisingly, is diabetes. A Toronto psychiatrist who is also a diabetic, Dr. John W. Lovett Doust, observed sadly, "We crave for love and we never will have enough love."

The love that doctors admire for its therapeutic properties —Sándor Ferenczi believed patients are healed by "physician's love"—isn't to be confused with the sugar display of pampering, overcoddling parents. Overprotectiveness is actually one of the nastier forms of hate and produces obese, depressed, illness-prone children.

Montreal psychiatrist Karl Stern stated that underloved children, since they can't mature past the infantile stage of passively receiving love, may grow up vulnerable to such character defects as delinquency, alcoholism and homosexuality. Lack of ability to love also shows itself in pseudosexuality by men and women who give no sweetness to the performance of sexual intercourse. Psychoanalyst Harry Stack Sullivan called it "instrumental masturbation" when the sex act is consummated without love.

One of the most troublesome side-effects of inability to love is the failure to discriminate in a choice of love sources. Teen-aged girls, in particular, are vulnerable to this lack of selectivity; their love-need is so clamorous they are easier to fool than a baby. Dr. Maslow paraphrases regretfully, "Nonlove makes us blind."

On the beneficial side, adults who can't love individuals sometimes strike up a monument of a love affair with the human race. It's a form of guilt-pacifying that psychiatrists crisply describe as sublimation. Philantropists who can't abide the society of anyone but bloodless servants are prime examples of this. So was Clara Barton, organizer of the American Red Cross, who rejected her suitor over and over because she felt incapable of love.

Others solve the problem in meaner ways, by loving intensely something apart from humanity. Misers are in this category, and so are work addicts. The most successful men and women in North America usually cannot love people, but only their jobs. A psychologist from United College, Professor John Clarke, told a Winnipeg audience, "I find that the kids with real difficulties often come from good homes. I think this is because insecure people don't develop their capacity for affection."

What meager warmth such people contain is sometimes lavished on budgies, or research, or stamp collections, or neatness. If they are married, this results in cool, lonely relationships lanced with argument. Psychiatrist Karl Menninger warns that a man who prefers a police dog to a son shouldn't be coaxed to change his mind. He is probably emotionally incapable of fatherhood and would botch it up.

Fiction and real life often ennoble individuals who declare they love but one person in all the world, an arrangement that seems to reflect a superior, discriminating ability to love. Psychologists are unimpressed. They say that such people reveal an inferior, rather than superior, capacity for love. One Big Love attachments are based in neurosis, the experts aver, with such poor specimens as an infantile person adhering to someone who prefers infants, a masochist clinging to someone who exploits him (delicious) or a sadist to someone whose overdeveloped guilt requires him to endure continuous punishment.

Mature love doesn't restrict itself to one person, or even to one family or one nation. It overflows in easy abundance, observing the Golden Rule without deliberating about it. It marks the dignity of every man and treasures the qualities of courage and honor. Genuine love respects every form of life, and this is the essence of morality.

Such generosity of love emanates only from people who

first of all love themselves. Without self-love, existence becomes a poignant search for flattery. "There is nothing more conducive to giving the child the experience of what love, joy and happiness are than being loved by a mother who loves herself," wrote psychoanalyst Erich Fromm.

There is a distinction between self-love and selfishness; they are, in fact, opposites. Self-love, or as Antoine de Saint-Exupéry put it, being one's own friend, is reflected in a dismissal of infantile self-preoccupation. Having accepted himself as not a bad egg, the individual is free of the encumbrances of behaving in a likable manner (a tedious business), sharply watching out for insults, constant worry that whatever shabby throne has been attained will be usurped. The mature, with their sense of worth snug in their souls, are inpregnable against adversity.

The selfish person, on the other hand, can't stop thinking about himself. "It isn't that he loves himself too much," wrote Dr. Fromm, "but too little. In fact, he hates himself." He must therefore grasp and devour every crumb of comfort he can obtain; in his misery, he must sacrifice his dearest child in the hope of improving his lot. Self-hatred is also the vile root of some displays of unselfishness. While the selfish person gives nothing to others, being barren, the "unselfish" person appears to give and give—relentlessly. The recipient is crushed, as he was meant to be. The martyr-mother, in particular, is a figure of death, putting such a burden of malicious goodness on her family that they can never be free of her. Her smothering concern and unctuous servitude are, according to Dr. Menninger, "more crippling than beatings and blows." For sons, martyr-mothers are a major cause of arrested masculinity.

Homosexuality is only one example of incomplete masculinity; promiscuity is another. Don Juan, celebrated in history as the world's greatest lover, goes into psychology textbooks as emotionally impotent. His conquests are regarded as acts of hatred against women, probably in revenge for his stonehearted mother who abandoned him at an early age.

The late Errol Flynn, a contemporary Don Juan, freely admitted that he loathed women; his mother detested him cordially from birth. Rapists also suffer from underdeveloped masculinity and so do fetishists, voyeurs and imitators of the Marquis de Sade. Mothers who hate their children, by no means an uncommon breed, inflict impotency that can be either physical or emotional.

Romantic love, erroneously epitomized by Don Juan, is the aspect of love most admired in the Western world. Its pursuit is the pedestal that maintains a billion-dollar traffic in mascara, moon-June music, mouthwash and padded brassières, but it finds few fanciers among the scientists. Ortega y Gasset described falling in love as "an inferior state of mind, a form of transitory imbecility." A thousand years ago, he was anticipated by the Moslem physician Avicenna, who firmly listed love with mental diseases.

Sexual drive and loneliness make it a simple matter to experience an anguish-glory sensation known as love. In this love-hungry age, the irresistible lure is to appear loving, a display in which smiles play a prominent part. The rest is a duplication of the love ritual of most feathered, furred or scaled creatures: the female is coquettishly helpless, which arouses the stalwart stallion in the man as surely as dawn stirs the mating instinct in pigeons. Men compete for women with such buck displays as convertibles, college degrees and crime—police statistics are fattened by men showing off. Women compete by a soft show of receptiveness.

In the process, immature people get their glasses steamed up and can't differentiate reality from illusion. Mature love contains sexual desire as one of its components, but sexual desire can exist without a shred of love being exchanged. It is perfectly possible to have a whopping sexual attraction between people who otherwise find one another irritating. Among the people most readily fooled by eroticism are those obsessed with the idea of love, desolate souls who yearn to be transported by it so piercingly that they can simulate its symptoms readily, as women longing for babies can wish themselves into morning sickness.

The selection of mates, psychologists believe, is almost puppetry controlled by unconscious childhood associations. For example, a woman who writhed under the domination of a severe father but had a friendly relationship with her brothers is likely to be revolted by harsh, masculine men and attracted by men whose less aggressive natures reproduce the happier fraternal camaraderie. A man whose mother was efficient and adamant, while his father was a Dagwood bumbler, won't be intrigued by fluttering femininity; well-organized and capable women like his mother are nurture's plan for him.

Such marriages work out as neatly as Euclid on paper, but in practice are tricky. Human beings are too complicated to be satisfied by one dimension of their needs; they don't want merely a replica or an antithesis of their parents, they want a *combination.* As children they were ambivalent about their parents and the uneasiness is projected into adult marriages. The woman in the example will also have a leftover taste for heavy-handed men; the man will discover that his boyhood exasperation at his mother's imperious instructions is reactivated, in spades, when his wife does it.

If the marriages result in divorce as a result of these conflicts, each partner will be at the mercy of his unconscious IBM selector again and may select another manifestation of the same person. One man, married for ten years to a flint-eyed tigress with a loud, coarse voice, abruptly divorced her and married a flint-eyed tigress with a low voice.

On the other hand, the second marriage may be a pure reaction against the first one. The daughter of the tyrant may turn in her weak husband for a tough one, who will infuriate her just as her father did, while the son of a dictatorial mother may demonstrate his severed umbilical cord by marrying a scatterbrain, who will horrify him.

An astute woman psychoanalyst, Joan Riviere, once mused, "How much does the need for reassurance about one's own value play a part in the decisions of men and women to marry, and how little does the feeling of love or sexual desire motivate them?"

The modern ideal of marriage, emphasizing such campfire virtues as co-operation, cheerfulness and friendship, serves to perpetuate many badly sorted partnerships. No love is exchanged, but only small talk, common interests and stale sex. Politeness without genuine concern is the art of insult. The effort of pretending to be agreeable and zestful, for the sake of peace, is so depleting of inner resources that a sense of being hollow results. The public relations approach to marriage is dehumanizing, and eventually produces two isolated, bitter beings, nursing their indigestible grudges.

Thinning emotions down to avoid a row—or self-disclosure —is a strangulation that puts the man or woman in peril of a breakdown. Some deal with the emptiness of such attenuated existences by having an affair, or moving to a new neighborhood, or changing jobs, or having a baby—but the distractions are temporary and the loneliness returns. Experts say that the core of the problem is a lack of self-love. Until the individual develops self-esteem, privately, unshakably, nothing on earth can make a dent in his aloneness.

"The variety of feelings and strivings that can be covered by the term love or that are subjectively felt as such is astonishing," commented psychoanalyst Karen Horney. "For the very reason that love in our civilization is so rarely a genuine affection, maltreatment and betrayal abound."

What *is* mature love? Oswald Schwartz writes: "To be in love means to be anchored in the safest anchorage, that is in complete union with another being. It means the opening up of unlimited horizons, and the extension of our existence far beyond the boundaries of our personality, it means richness and fullness through fulfillment."

Mature love can grow, observes Walter Lippmann, because its object is not the mere relief of physical tension, "but all the objects with which the two lovers are concerned. They desire their worlds in each other, and therefore their love is as interesting as their worlds and their worlds are as interesting as their love.''

Erich Fromm devised a definition of mature love, breaking it into four characteristics: responsibility, care, respect and knowledge. The heart of love, he says, is that the partners preserve each other's integrity. He echoes Benedict Spinoza, who wrote three hundred years ago that married love should have as its source freedom of mind.

Without this condition, the union is a legalized persecution.

The transformation that people want marriage to make in their lives is the child's game of expecting a gift for being good. It is a reflection of the standard North American technique of using love as a disciplinarian tool, granting it to their children for obedience, high marks or cleanliness and withholding it for untidy bedrooms or sassiness. Marriage, the supremely good deed, accordingly should be rewarded with infinite, unfaltering, forgiving love, only forever.

It is true for one couple in a hundred, approximately the proportion of mature adults in our society. Only they have the secret: "Love and you shall be loved," said Emerson.

The relationship between man and God is also determined by how much maturity each man can bring to it. Freud declared that religion is a neurosis, conjured up cleverly by man's fear of being alone in the universe. Others see religion as a real bulwark against mankind's major fear—each person's terror of the dark, unpredictable stranger within. The mood of Christianity has been traced through the Old Testament's God of hard tasks and wrath to the New Testament's compassionate, gentle God. This progression, some say, duplicates the infant's first view of the world as harsh, powerful and arbitrary, followed by the young child's partial independence of his mother's embrace, except when he is hurt or frightened.

Religion in mature people goes a step beyond the Father-God and the Mother-God—and beyond the adolescent stage of atheism—to achieve the Within-God. Having respect for themselves, they can respect God and merge the two in a oneness that the Buddhists revere as a private experience and the Christians and Jews as a radiance to be shared. Oneness with God, which causes the individual to be as divinely loving and just as the size of his soul permits, is the comprehension of the simple truth: God is love. The finest wisdom of which man is capable, it has been achieved only rarely in the past two thousand years. Nietzsche claimed that the last Christian died on the cross.

It is not, however, unknown. Nearly three hundred years ago, an English statesman, Joseph Addison, asked the physician Sir Samuel Garth what religion he was. Garth answered, "Wise men all hold the same religion." And when Addison inquired what this religion was, Garth serenely informed him, "Wise men never tell."

Today's religious revival has something in common with the spirit of good-sportsmanship that pervades modern marriages. Theologians and psychologists alike are concerned that the emphasis on the social benefits of religion is the product of the collapse of belief. Many adults find it impossible to be confident that there is life after death; it doesn't seem likely, either, that God is interested, or aware, of their problems. They attend services therefore with a tiny hope of getting back their faith, but mostly because of its advertised benefits: self-improvement instruction, business and community contacts, increased self-esteem.

The late philosopher Carl Jung once said, "Theology does not help those who are looking for the key, because theology demands faith and faith cannot be made: it is in the truest sense a gift of grace."

Faith isn't an ornament of the personality, but a quality close to courage that moves out gamely. It flowers of its own accord with maturity, and won't be hurried no matter how urgent the need. Children learn it first by observing that the mother who goes out of the house always returns to them and that all their hurts eventually heal. Faith is the fundamental stabilizer in society; without faith in strangers every man would have to be armed. Love is impossible without faith, since all love is a risky business, a gut-exposure that invites disembowelment.

Hope is also associated with love, but provokes controversy. Albert Camus called it a negation of life and vitality, since it waits on the future, the last and greatest of the human afflictions released by Pandora. But the nineteenth-century Swiss philosopher of loneliness, Henri-Frédéric Amiel, believed that everything in life is based on hope. "All the activities of man presuppose a hope in him of attaining an end. Once kill this hope and his movements become senseless, spasmodic and convulsive." Adult ability to hope for improved conditions in the midst of poverty or tragedy is often rooted in childhood longings; too much early frustration can permanently wound the ability to be optimistic.

Evil or not, hope has enormous influence. Its major testimonial is the advertising industry, a pure extension of the child's world of wishful thinking.

Friendship, a shape of love that involves both faith and hope, was regarded by Aristotle as the noblest of the external aids to happiness, but he added the warning that the man who has many friends has no friend. Psychiatrist Karl Menninger agrees. Since most friendships are sustained when one of the friends has an uncritical, supporting nature toward the other, "there is a limit to the number of friendships" that can be maintained.

Montreal psychiatrist Alastair MacLeod once wrote that variety is as important in friendships as it is in diet. He recommended the inclusion of a boring friend and an annoying friend, as a sort of calisthenic to keep the personality from becoming flabby.

It is only in recent generations that so much has been expected of the emotion of love. The notion of mutual gratification, giving and dignity is a modern concoction, unheard of in past centuries. There was no trace of even affection in the mating of the aboreal pre-man. Anthropologist Weston La Barre explains that the male hung around the female not because of her attractiveness but because he had a genetically selected all-year-round sexual interest in her.

There is some doubt that this early female had any emotional attachment to her young. Modern infants have a strong enough grasp at birth to support their own weight, suggesting that they once survived abandonment by clinging to their mothers, who would tolerate the passengers in order to relieve the congestion of milk in their breasts.

This rough version of togetherness somehow launched the human family, but the dawn of written history found little improvement in its cosiness. Laborers hand-raised their children and depended on the co-operation of their wives, but the mark of elegance for centuries was the cloistered and ignored wife and infants given to servants to nurse and raise. The Greeks, for instance, regarded wives as dowry-equipped breeders. For sexual pleasure they visited brothels and for intellectual stimulation joined the salons of cultured, charming prostitutes. Love was reserved for the sexual feeling mature men had for young boys, which is what Plato intended by the word—a far cry from the present understanding of platonic love.

The Christian concept of brotherly love caused such confusion that centuries passed before gentleness, justice and sympathy gained much respect. The brutality of early Christians, the Crusaders and the Spanish Inquisitors, is an infamy, but modern churchmen are still disgracing themselves—a bishop in Spain blessed the guns of a firing squad, ministers in the U. S. South bar Negroes from their pews and Rome failed to declare itself publicly against the slaughter of Jews in Germany or Buddhists in Saigon.

Possibly because of the chastity of Jesus Christ, the enjoyment of sex has been considered something of a blasphemy for two thousand years. For a time, early in Christianity, an unconsummated marriage was the ideal. The strangest variation of this occurred during the century of the Crusades, when even adultery wasn't always consummated. Knights and errant ladies lay naked together, with a drawn sword between

them as a reminder. Currently, such brinkmanship morality
is still practiced as a conscience sop. In colleges it is known
as the "all but" chastity technique.

The development of love went through a period of idealized
misery during the feudal era, when sorrow thrilled, eroticism
was stifled and hopeless love was the best kind. The trouba-
dours composed swooning love songs, suggesting that the excitement of being enchanted by beauty or manliness was the
principle benefit to be derived from being human. André
Maurois reflected disgustedly, "We owe to the Middle Ages
the two worst inventions of humanity—romantic love and
gunpowder."

The Reformation lifted the weight of guilt and sin from the
marriage bed. The Puritans, according to Morton M. Hunt
in *The Natural History of Love*, were the first to regard wives
with sentiments new in the world, tenderness and concern.
The Victorians, repelled by the sordid business practices of
the industrial era, advanced family life by all but deifying
their homes as bowers where they could freshen their dignity. The formality of the family was shaken at the turn of
the century by Freud's condemnation of sex repression,
shaken again by the emancipation of women, shaken until it
reeled under the anxieties, loneliness and expectations of the
nuclear age.

The family of today is unparalleled in the history of man.
Never before has such an overwhelming proportion of parents
been so dedicated to their children, so resolute in family shar-
ing of goods and leisure. Love is venerated: parents attempt
to love their children correctly, as scientists suggest, not too
much and not too little, and to love one another smoothly.
They know everything about it—how beneficial it is, what it
says, what it looks like. They know everything but how to
love.

The key is self-respect. It is a magic glass slipper that can
whisk an existence from the scullery of desolation and guilt
to the ballroom, where the mature elite are enjoying themselves. The miracle of life is that most people are capable

of becoming emotionally mature. They succeed by forcing themselves to forgive more easily, doubt less readily; steady themselves inside and demonstrate tact outside. They establish order in their lives and find time to meditate in solitude, time for friendships, time for hard work and time to be gay.

It's quiet growth, but beautiful. A research psychologist who spent twenty years studying adults has remarked, "I have come to the conclusion that maladjustment is never inevitable and that it is not unrealistic to think that a man is capable of being responsible for himself."

The development of a skill in love has never been more urgent. Dr. Jung wrote: "It would be very much in the interest of free society to give some thought to the question of human relationship . . . Where love stops, power begins, and violence, and terror."

CHAPTER TWO

Everyone Hates, Including
Mothers, Lovers and Patriots

Hate is the underlying emotion of most men. In greater or lesser quantities, people hate all their lives. Freud believed that mankind is inherently destructive and love is a faked attitude; he called humanity a "gang of murderers." Modern psychiatrists have come to believe in love, but they note that even mature, loving adults seem to need something to hate, or some hate-substitute such as golf or spring cleaning. Karl Menninger, one of the best known of United States psychiatrists, considers self-hatred so integral a part of everyone's character that "in the end each man kills himself in his own selected way, fast or slow, soon or late."

Humanists observe the same behavior and find opposite causes. They believe that babies are naturally full of goodness and love and begin to hate only when their mothers are slow to feed them or change icy diapers. Hate, by this definition, is a form of self-preservation, since the baby is reacting to the threat against his true self, his essential lovableness.

Whatever the interpretation, hate gets the personality moving. Without hate, humans would languish all their lives in a warm stupor of passive contentment; without hate, they would need no companion but mother, since mother would be perfect. Juggling love and hate, toddlers rapidly learn it is discreet to hide the hate. Few adults hate openly, many believe they don't hate at all. What mankind hates most of all is hatred.

The most common disguise is to pretend that hatred is merely the justified return of someone else's hatred, a process known to psychiatry as projection. The ideal subject for this invention is a stranger, which gives rise to the kind of hallucination that simplifies life for generals, munition manufacturers and rabble-rousers.

"It is possible to be fiercely partisan only against those who are wholly alien," Walter Lippmann once wrote. "When an agitator wishes to start a crusade, a religious revival, an inquisition, or some sort of jingo excitement, the further he goes from the centers of modern civilization the more following he can attract."

Historians have long been intrigued by the frequency with which hysterical paranoids, some of them clearly insane, are able to sway entire countries into the mass paranoia that festers rapidly into war, each citizen convinced that he is hated and threatened by citizens of another country. Psychiatrists explain that the nucleus of hate in everyone makes it easy to lead a nation into mass madness. There is within us all a demented savage who enjoys killing.

"In the end," comments Karl Stern, Montreal's illustrious psychiatrist-writer, "hatred becomes a strange bond of union." It's even a happy fraternity: neurotics feel much better when hate can be called patriotism and displayed openly.

Mental hospitals all over Europe, South and North America have noticed that paranoics, whose most notable symptom is their belief that everyone, everywhere hates them, name the same four primary sources of their imagined persecution: Jews, Freemasons, Communists and the Roman Catholic

Church. Interestingly, the same selection favored by lunatics is also prominent in the hate platforms of such extremist organizations as the John Birchers.

Some targets, on the other hand, are devised from materials at hand. In the southern United States, poor whites are weirdly comforted by hating Negroes, just as the Germans beaten in World War I were able to regain their battered pride by refining anti-Semitism.

Studies of prejudice demonstrate that specific hatreds are usually chosen as a matter of convenience. A hate-filled person concentrates on the minority at hand, and feels unburdened in direct ratio to the amount of hatred he feels is safe to demonstrate. Lower levels of life show the same trend. Cichlids, a perchlike tropical fish, is friendly with his mate only so long as he keeps encountering another male cichlid that he can scowl at. Even a mirror in his aquarium makes a suitable substitute. But if the other cichlids are removed, or the mirror becomes dirty, the essentially nasty cichlid promptly eats his mate. Certainly the families of bigots would suffer if all the neighbors moved a hundred miles away.

The late Carl G. Jung was convinced that the only solution to individual hatred lies in a personal and honest inspection of one's own behavior, and acknowledgment of every evil thus discovered. The purpose is not to wipe out hatred, which is an impossibility, but to hate correctly. Healthy hate—what psychoanalyst Erich Fromm calls "reactive hate"—is based on a respect for life and erupts whenever life is abused. Decency could not exist without this kind of hate.

The wrong kind of hate, irrational hate, most often stems from a mood of revenge and few people are mature enough to be without some vengeance. It has its genesis in infancy, when even the most attentive, loving mother arouses hatred in her infant when she doesn't feed him the instant he is hungry. Later he learns to hate the rest of the family for diverting his mother's attention from him.

His hate shows itself in destructiveness with toys, and in biting and pinching, which the Freudians claim is intended murder. For this reason the smallest baby knows that hating is wrong—not as an ethical distinction but because when carried to its logical conclusion (the death of the mother) it will jeopardize the baby's existence.

He begins anxiously to uncover objects he can hate enthusiastically without the risk of being orphaned. Unpopular teachers or odd playmates serve this function, providing targets which are guilt-free because the group approves hating them. Such a heavy investment of hate needs a balance of relatively pure love, by which psychiatrists explain the rapture preadolescents feel toward their idols.

The push and pull between love and hate in childhood evolves into the moral code of the adult. Hate always provokes guilt, unless it is sanctioned by society, so the growing child steers his course by means of hate. He avoids those acts which cause him to hate himself or feel guilty, as well as he is able, and so arrives at a conscience.

A healthy conscience, one not unrealistically loaded with ideas of sin and unworthiness or one that is not infantilely weak, depends almost entirely on the direction hate takes. If it turns inward, to self-hate, the personality is doomed to a lifelong hair shirt. "Good" children, denied all expressions of hatred, develop heavy puritanical consciences which are among the finest hating instruments known to man. No one is more viciously against pleasure for others than a man who forces himself to live austerely.

Hate *must* be used up. Children, for instance, literally can run hate off, punishing their bodies with exhaustion and their enemies with defeat. Team games provide splendid, group-endorsed hate regulators. Bedridden children relish toy soldiers or competitive games. Children who can work off their hatred successfully are then released from it to appreciate goodness. Little boys cheer heros and small girls play nurse.

Later on, as teen-agers, they are almost certain to make an unholy mess of their loving and hating. Engrossed as they are with crushes and a dawning skill for friendships, they have few places to put their hate but back on their parents, a normal technique of maturing that is never wildly popular with parents. Psychoanalyst Melanie Klein once commented, "There are children who can keep love and admiration for their parents through this stage, but it isn't very common."

The amount of hate in every human personality isn't fixed, as the number of eyes and ears is. The hate mass is formed during a baby's first two years and its size depends on the amount of genuine affection the baby receives and how much independence he is permitted. Totally unloved babies experience total hatred. An important experiment in Detroit in 1946 dealt with a group of boys of ten years of age who had been disliked by their parents and love-starved from birth. These children, confirmed criminals and savage as jungle animals, are described in a remarkable book, *Children Who Hate*, by Fritz Redl and David Wineman, who supervised them for nineteen months in a residence supported by the Junior League.

"No one, not parents, brothers, neighbors, uncles, friends, cousins, took any interest in them," wrote the authors. "This whole vacuum in adult relationship potentialities cannot possibly be over-estimated in terms of how impoverished these children felt or how much hatred and suspicion they had toward the adult world."

The normal child who is frustrated in something he wants, such as going to a movie, feels a quick welling up of hatred. It subsides as his mind turns to other projects that he has enjoyed and he begins to plan a substitute activity. Moping is one of hatred's many faces and the average child sulks a bit but can get over his mood fairly quickly. The hate-filled children in Detroit, however, couldn't overcome the initial flood of fury because they couldn't remember ever having a good time. Every frustration provoked a terrifying, blood-vengeance tantrum that spent itself only in destruction. A pathetic symptom of their emotional malnutrition was their positive zest for parrying the hatred they encountered in most adults and their alarm, confusion and dismay when the psychologists persisted in being affectionate.

It is contentious whether watching violence on television or in movies or following sports that feature mayhem relieves hate or stimulates it. It probably varies, even within the individual personality. Sometimes a husband mildly churned up because of his wife's nagging comes home in a soothed state of mind after exhorting his team to kill the opposition; the same man, in a darker mood, may identify with a victim being savagely beaten and will hate more intensely the next person who offends him. Psychologists feel that mild doses of physical roughness are harmless, or even beneficial, but sadism breeds sadism in the onlooker—as history amply demonstrates.

Some hate outlets are surprising. Most forms of play are hate-releasing, even quiet games such as parcheesi. Bridge is particularly aggressive and Karl Menninger calls poker a fighting game. Chess, according to the legend, was devised by the Buddhists as a substitute for war.

Harvard's great philosopher-psychologist, William James, first advanced the theory that work is also a moral equivalent for war. At work, he said, a man is pitted against a force that must be battled and mastered. Whether he is a stevedore, comedian, salesman or teacher, he has an adversary to match himself against daily. The housewife who attacks her scrubbing vigorously uses up hate by turning it against dirt and disorder; frantically tidy women are revealing that they carry more hate than they can handle.

One theory of hate, the Freudian one, maintains that mankind's goodness stems from a contrived disguise of vileness. By this he explained the frequent choice of first-born children for some selfless vocation such as medicine or education; the extra jealousy they feel toward the younger brothers and sisters who usurp their exclusive claim to parental attention is compensated, in their private scale of good and evil, by a life of service.

Freud wrote: "It is interesting to learn that the existence of strong 'bad' impulses in infancy is often the actual condition for an unmistakable inclination toward 'good' in the

adult person. Those who have as children been the most pronounced egoists may well become the most helpful and self-
sacrificing members of the community; most of our senti-
mentalists, friends of humanity, champions of animals have
been evolved from little sadists and animal-tormentors."

Many modern psychiatrists believe that Freud was wrong
about hate and that this makes him wrong about a lot of
other things. The Scot, Ian D. Suttie, complained in *The
Origins of Love and Hate,* "Freudian theory is based on hate.
Freud's own childish rage and despair find expression in anti-
feminism, the subjection of love to sex, the acclamation of
hate and aggression as universal—a complete social pessi-
mism." Milder dissenters conclude that Freud was half
right: good behavior probably stems in part from a sublimation of inner evil. There is inescapable evidence, however,
that every living person has a supply of genuine, spontaneous
goodness.

Since goodness isn't plentiful, most people have a great deal
of hatred to disperse. Some will make a show of loving-kind-
ness, going through the motions of a generous attachment to
another person. The true nature of their "love" is revealed to
be well laced with hatred whenever a small disagreement
turns up; deep malice makes an insult mortally accurate.
People who kill the one they love, as Elizabeth I did the
Earl of Essex and Henry II did Thomas à Becket, are displaying the ultimate marbling of love with hate. The geno-
cidal Adolf Eichmann also exhibited grotesque ambivalence—
in his youth he was attracted strongly to Judaism, relished
Jewish food, had many Jewish friends and learned some of the
language.

Sometimes the leakage of foulness in the personality can be
made to seem virtuous. Justice makes an effective mask for
mean dispositions. Moral judgments are a particularly satisfying form of hatred and so are the righteous punishments
meted out thumpingly by judges, teachers, clergymen or
parents, who piously declare themselves to be upholding law,
education, religion and character building. It is interesting

that martyrs often evince malevolence toward their families, while inspiring strangers with the depth of their love for a cause. A conspicuous case in point is that of John Brown, the abolitionist who fought slavery for twenty years while his wife and childen suffered starvation and madness. His grown sons were slaughtered in battle under his command.

High principles are an ingenious disguise for hatred. Scientists, financiers, politicians and zealot housewives with meetings to attend all neglect their families in the name of higher good. To psychologists, the higher good served is the maintenance of a false self-image. Dedication is often a mantle to conceal a poor ability to love and a fine talent for hating. "The pretense of honesty and fairness," writes psychoanalyst Karen Horney, "is most frequently found in the aggressive type, especially when he has marked sadistic tendencies."

Some kinds of humor, particularly practical jokes and the character assassination known jovially as ribbing, contain a great deal of hate. Comedians are among the most desolate, grievance-full men in the entertainment business, while wits are often gloomy, merciless people. Dean Swift, whose *Gulliver's Travels* is still the most savage satire in English, said he only laughed twice in his life. He was so consumed with hate that he urged his countrymen in Ireland to burn everything that came from England except the coal.

Students of theology cannot avoid the strong element of hate in every religion. In some cases, a separate and distinct hate object—such as the devil—is sharply defined, a psychologically sound practice which allows a more generous love for the good god. Religions which don't have a devil often develop a fallible god instead, whose faults can be disliked. Almost every religion includes some form of satisfying ceremonial killing, refined in Christianity to the eating of flesh and blood symbolically at Communion.

Hate is vital to worship, but even more powerful a factor in flattery. Enthusiastic fans who slavishly imitate an idol's mannerisms and dress usually harbor a staggering amount of

envy and are delighted to discover a flaw that justifies top-
pling him. This human proclivity accounts for the otherwise
bewildering overnight reversals of public opinion of its most
exalted leaders. Conversely, the death of a leader instantly relieves the hatred, leaving only love. "A fallen leader," Freud
observed laconically, "is often deified by the mob that killed
him."

Hate is also a frightful coward. It was Charles Darwin who
discerned that hatred of a superior adversary usually converts
itself to fear, while hatred of an inferior one rapidly becomes
anger.

Hate, however it shows itself irrationally, is always the out-
growth of self-hatred. The less emotionally mature the individual, the more he hates. Hatred apparently is the lowest,
most primeval aspect of man. But hating oneself is such a
painful experience that people generally protect themselves
from knowing about it. They employ ingenious ruses: they
may become martyrs, or else monumentally, punitively unselfish, or else overwork in the muddled hope of simultaneously improving their self-esteem and killing themselves.
Their lives are ground to bitterness with depression and the
sense of being incompetent. Suicides among gloriously successful people, or those who seem so, have been explained as
due to the sudden failure of their rationalization. Popularity
or perpetual motion or whatever technique has been employed
to divert attention from a basic self-hatred is a flimsy device;
when it fails to work, the self-loathing spills out.

Self-hate relentlessly seeks the death of the person, one way
or another. Alcoholism, accident-proneness, hypochondria, excessive smoking, chronic overexertion, peevish sensitivity, all
are forms of self-mutilation. There are nearly a hundred suicides a day in North America that can be readily identified
as such; no one can estimate how many true suicides are concealed among the victims of accident or illness.

According to Erich Fromm, hate and destructiveness are
the outcome of an unlived life. Hate is deathlike even in its
physical symptoms; it is the strangler among emotions. It has

been noted, principally by psychoanalyst Joan Riviere, that babies are in pain when they hate because their screaming chokes them and stomach cramps and scalding evacuations combine to cause agony. Similarly, adults are in pain when they hate, the more acute because social strictures demand that they scream silently and endure internal breakdown rather than risk being unlikable.

A hating person has the sensation of struggling against a clamp, whose rigidity is the result of his own inability to un-bend and love. The emotion of hate roils and burns within whatever personal containment the person's family and oc-cupation demands. As a result, many mild, gentle, reserved people develop high blood pressure and heart disease, which some doctors ascribe purely to their self-contempt.

Carl G. Jung once noted sadly, "Since it is universally be-lieved that man is merely what his consciousness knows of itself, he regards himself as harmless and so adds stupidity to iniquity. . . . The evil that comes to light in man and that undoubtedly dwells within him is of gigantic proportions."

This evil must be dealt with, not only because it is the very condition of all unhappiness but also because it can de-stroy the world. Mean nationalism and bigoted patriotism are the faces of mass hatred. When it is really out for blood, hate always calls itself love and takes care to carry a flag. All those who butcher other human beings do so in the name of country or religion. Voltaire wrote bitterly, "It is forbidden to kill; therefore all murderers are punished unless they kill in large numbers and to the sound of trumpets." Currently a Trappist monk, Thomas Merton, sanely and desperately is trying to combat a rather widespread theory in the radical right that Christianity will be advanced if thermonuclear war is launched. He is the author of a stunning series of essays in leading Roman Catholic journals.

With humanity still so far short of its potential faith and compassion, it may be true that the world keeps its equilib-rium only by hating. This sort of sickly balance has been observed in the microcosm of individual families. Psychia-

trists and social workers in Montreal have drawn wide attention to their studies of entire families, which they find often
need a black sheep. The offensive member draws off all the
family's venom, enabling them to get along better with one
another. If the errant member reforms, the family then is
profoundly disturbed and begins to fall apart. In the same
way, nations perhaps need a blackguard country to hate. If
an old enemy has the bad form to sign a peace pact, most
countries show considerable enterprise in lining up a new
threatening nation.

Nevertheless, the study of man shows a general advance in
humaneness. It is a process that can be accelerated, the
philosophers say, only by the increase of love in the world.
Hate diminishes exactly as love expands. Buddhists are taught
that "hatred does not cease by hatred, but only by love," a
theory shared by the seventeenth-century philosopher Benedict Spinoza, who noted that hatred is enlarged when it is met
by an opposing hate and therefore, logically, would wither if
it met affection. He added firmly that men who display smiles
and love when they encounter hate will enjoy themselves
hugely, "and scarcely need at all the help of fortune."

In modern times, the United States Negro is attempting to
meet hatred if not with love, then at least with heroic passivity. It derives much from such staunch declarations as that
of the Negro educationist, Booker T. Washington, who said,
"I shall never permit myself to stoop so low as to hate any
man."

Recent psychiatric investigations point up the dichotomy
of man, inescapably both a lover and a colossal hater. It is
felt that the first step toward control of the lurking, demented
brute within every man, is to acknowledge its existence and
recognize its many disguises. Hate's preservative is its ability
to pretend to be some other worthier emotion.

Once identified, hate can be put to work. The earth abounds
in targets. A man in charge of himself hates hypocrisy, he
hates abuse, he hates despots. Mohandas Gandhi in 1920

stated simply, "I am anti-untruth, anti-humbug and anti-injustice."

It is a hopeful sign that men who have subjected themselves to such humiliating and honest introspection have emerged as improved personalities. A bizarre example of such self-change is provided by a survey of wife-murderers serving life sentences in Quebec prisons. McGill University's Bruno W. Cormier, the psychiatrist in charge of the study, reported that the men had been so shocked by their own violence that they were brought to a stark self-evaluation. Dr. Cormier found them "greatly changed for the better."

Dr. Jung believed stoutly that any one who found the courage to judge his own content would then find less hate in the world, since hate tends to imagine hate everywhere, and would be able then to love more truly. "As a man is," William Blake once wrote, "so he sees."

Including even Dr. Cormier's murderers, anyone who can soften his own personality fits John Dewey's definition of virtue: "A good man is the man who, no matter how morally unworthy he has been, is moving to become better."

CHAPTER THREE

Fear Increases Sexual Desire

Fear is the paralyzing emotion. In 1943, fear alone killed two hundred people in a London bomb shelter. None were even bruised. A bomb struck near by, the lights went out and they simply stopped breathing. Fear is the sole cause of voodoo deaths as well. Less sensationally, civilized people die by degrees because they are afraid constantly of ill health or misfortune.

While normal fear is the preservative that compels a man to save his skin if he can, any abnormal fear is a wound that will make his character mean and exhaust his heart, stomach and digestion. Fear can control an entire nation. Huge populations are docile under small occupation forces, if they are afraid; currently fear contributes to the passivity with which the world watches the approach of nuclear war.

Most adult fears are so easy for a psychiatrist to unravel that they are something of a parlor game. Fear of aging, for instance, is related to the fear of impotence; fear of death is most acute in people who fear life and live it tremulously; fear of the dark is derived from fear of being isolated, since children customarily are separated from their parents at night; fear of burglars is a groove in memory made by a magnified childhood fear.

Many other fears are really fears of revealing one's true nature: fear of guns, experienced so violently that soldiers have committed suicide rather than handle live ammunition, is sometimes a fear of giving in to the unacknowledged longing to kill.

More than forty years ago, a psychologist at Johns Hopkins University, Dr. John B. Watson, performed a number of fear-inducing experiments on an unfortunate nine-month-old-baby named Albert. Like all babies, Albert wasn't concerned when a fluffy white rat was placed near him. He was even intrigued and reached to touch the animal, whereupon Dr. Watson struck a steel bar clangorously with a hammer right behind Albert. The baby screamed, then calmed down and reached for the animal again; Dr. Watson repeated the noise. Within a week, Albert was terrified of the rat and would crawl away howling. Eventually he was afraid of everything furry—dogs, cats, a fur coat, a ball of wool.

Many authorities believe that *all* human fears are conditioned by some means similar to Albert's experience. Some planted fears are necessary for survival, of course: respectful fear of traffic, for instance, of fire, stormy water, precipices. But babies soak up dozens more useless and damaging fears from their environment, mainly from mothers. The contagion of showing a baby fear reactions during a thunderstorm is well known and modern mothers endeavor gallantly to say, "See the pretty lightning?" They are less aware that babies also pick up adult nervousness at entertaining guests and adult consternation during injuries and fevers. A lifelong fear can be branded into a young brain in an instant. Ernest Jones, one of the world's most renowned psychoanalysts, once treated a man almost incapacitated by his fear of heights. He discovered that at the age of three the patient's crying had annoyed a boarder, who then held him by his heels over a cask of water and threatened to drop him if he wasn't quiet.

Some people contain much more fear than others. They are therefore panic-spreaders, a potential menace to the life and sanity of a community. Armies try to keep them out of battle areas; England put thousands of fear-carriers in work battalions behind the lines. Psychologists distinguish dangerously fearful persons by their unstable personalities, whose most common sympton is profound bigotry. Prejudice is the product of pure fear. Superpatriots and the unpatriotic both demonstrate fear of their fellow man to almost a lunatic degree.

Fear, even the fear of strangers, has in its essence a premonition of pain. Extreme fear accordingly brings on a protective deathlike state, resembling the device used by those living fossils, opossums. Its silence is eerie. A doctor who arrived on the scene of a train wreck only ten minutes after it occurred heard nothing but the murmurings of pastoral animals, though a hundred people were strewn about. The two hundred who died of fright in the London bomb shelter made no sound; mutism is not an uncommon symptom of terror.

Doctors are undecided about the progress of a fatal fear through the human body. Some believe that the victim dies of the disastrous drop in his blood pressure and others suspect he dies of smothering, his chest muscles so rigid that he can't breath. The surviving member of the original Siamese twins died of fright in 1874, a few hours after his brother died quietly in his sleep of a blood clot on his brain. Doctors who examined the twins found that the one who panicked had an "extended bladder which seemed to point to a severe disturbance of the emotional system."

In the yogi-like state of cataleptic fear the heart scarcely beats, there is little breathing and no hunger. Thirst, however, becomes acute. A man who believed he was about to be shot by bandits later reported, "My tongue began to swell and my mouth to get dry. This thirst rapidly became worse until my tongue clove to the roof of my mouth and I could scarcely get my breath."

Along with thirst are assorted disorders, all of which have been mocked by clowns: the face relaxes, the eyebrows raise, the eyes widen (according to Charles Darwin, to enable a man to see his adversary better); blood rushes away from the skin, leaving it pale and covered with a clammy sweat because the glands are out of kilter. There is a tendency to yawn. Vascular convulsions cause shivering, chattering teeth, gooseflesh and the sensation of hair standing on end. A Sutherland Highlanders' sergeant in the relief of Lucknow discovered by the light of a flaming torch that he was standing ankle-deep in loose gunpowder and later declared that his hair raised the bonnet from his head.

Stark fear can cause fainting, permanent paralysis, seizures, mental disturbances, premature aging and, as mentioned, death. Dr. Arthur Epstein of Tulane University has been studying epileptics and in 1963 reported his opinion that fear can break down healthy brain tissue. Among his examples was the case of a thirteen-year-old girl who was chased by a bulldog and subsequently had nightmares of running away from a mad dog. Ten months after the original fright, nighttime *grand mal* seizures began.

The most excruciating fear is experienced by those who must endure it without being able to escape or give it a battle. The shelling of trenches during the first World War broke the sanity and health of thousands. Whenever there is a possibility of either flight or fight, however, fear converts into almost exhilarating energy. It begins with a swift flood of adrenalin and sugar, stepping up the heartbeat and overfeeding the muscles so they won't feel fatigue. Blood shifts away from the stomach and intestines to the heart, brain and limbs, where it is needed most. Deeper, quicker breathing provides extra oxygen which enables the brain to concentrate beyond its normal power, and perhaps accounts for the unforgettable quality of a fearful experience.

There are some subtle, prehistoric alterations: blood undergoes a chemical change to make it coagulate more readily in case of a wound; sphincter muscles relax, emptying bowel and bladder to make the body light, and the digestive process halts in order not to distract the total effort that the mind and limbs are enabled to make.

An athlete recounts how, as an eleven-year-old boy being pursued by a bull, he cleared a fence and ditch that he wasn't able to jump again until he was a man. The brain and reflexes are so accelerated, in fact, that all other activity is by contrast in slow motion. A man whose car went out of control on the edge of a steep drop related later that the car seemed to pause while he unhurriedly took the precautions that saved his life—turning the wheels so the car pointed straight down the embankment and therefore didn't roll, switching off the ignition to prevent fire and stretching himself out on the floor under the dashboard.

Some people are afraid all the time. They stew about losing their job, their hair, their virility. The mindless reflexes nevertheless make the same adjustment to nebulous fear as it does to the approach of tigers, racing every engine in its arsenal. The chronically afraid suffer from diarrhea, inability to control urine, poor digestion, heart complaints, too vivid an imagination, sleeplessness and muscular tension, until the part of the person most affected wears out and collapses. A. M. Meerloo, a Dutch psychiatrist who reports on fear in *Patterns of Panic,* observes: "In periods of latent panic, people go more frequently to the cardiologist than to the psychologist."

Fear is very close to anger. Physiologically they are almost identical and anger accordingly often operates as an outlet for fear. It was observed during the last war that displaced children in camps throughout England rarely showed any fright during bombings but were constantly irritable, displaying tantrums over trivia. Similarly, a cornered animal or man is first frightened and then may marshal himself to be dangerously furious.

One of the oddest side-effects of fear is that it increases sexual desire. Psychiatrists believe that danger causes men and women to seek a physical union, both as a comfort and to assure themselves that they are powerful. Neurotic fearfulness often seeks for confidence by means of frequent sexual relationships.

Fear has a whiplash reaction that can mutilate the human mind long after the crisis is passed. Some of the calmest survivors of Rotterdam, for instance, labored for weeks after the ruthless bombing attacks, stoically setting up relief committees and finding homes for themselves. Their work done, they collapsed abruptly and had to be treated in mental hospitals. After such disasters as Boston's Cocoanut Grove dance hall fire of twenty years ago or Springhill, Nova Scotia's mine cave-in tragedy, psychologists observe that some of the strongest survivors and relatives paid for their control later by becoming ill and hysterical.

Many normal, seemingly stable people commit suicide after an earthquake or flood, unable to tolerate their fright; others become permanently insane. During the vicious bombings of Cologne in 1942, many unharmed Germans deliberately drowned themselves in the river.

Following a panic, the over-readied body remains tense for many days. The skin is pale and the temper exceedingly testy. In children there is a marked regression to baby ways, such as bed-wetting and thumb-sucking. Adults regress almost as transparently; they prattle, crave sweets, want to be pampered and sleep curled in the fetal position.

During the period of fear, human behavior is sometimes decidedly odd. There may be a withdrawal from reality, which performs a service to the overwrought mind that is as effective as a faint. Told the house is burning down, some will straighten a lampshade. Jewish women being collected for trips to concentration camps would ask permission to finish the dusting. Nervous adults clean their fingernails, sort the contents of their handbags, make irrelevant lists. The tactic isn't unknown in the animal world. Naturalists have observed "displacement activities" among some species of birds who, when attacked, busily start assembling nest materials.

Another technique of avoiding the full realization of a danger is to go to sleep. Just before a television appearance, many people are surprised to find themselves yawning. Apathy is a particularly destructive element in long-term fears, neutralizing humanity. This was particularly noticeable in occupied countries during the last war in Europe, when most people were indifferent to the disappearance of neighbors, and in Japanese prison camps, where only superb men lifted themselves above passivity. During the last war, underground workers warned that the Gestapo was coming sometimes were so paralyzed by their terror that they couldn't plan an escape and instead waited quietly to be arrested.

By one method or another, it is possible to get accustomed to a fear that doesn't go away, until finally its removal is alarming. Citizens of Dover, under intermittent bombardment from guns across the Channel for years, suffered "nerve-flop" when the shells ceased. They flocked to their doctors, complaining of exhaustion, insomnia and a vague sense of impending doom.

Mild fear, in fact, is so enjoyable that it is the foundation of many commercial successes. Midway rides and horror movies cater to the human relish for the thrill sensation of a stepped-up metabolism. There are also enthusiasts for such fear sports as skiing, racing and mountain climbing and such fear activities as gambling, cheating and cuckoldry. Children even are titillated by small doses of fear, squealing delightedly at jack-in-the-box, hide-and-seek and ghost stories. Many performers and after-dinner speakers seek audiences, although well aware that they will suffer nauseous stage fright. Fear seduces, as people who have stood by the glossy green brink of Niagara Falls can testify.

Newborn babies are the only fearless human beings. When the infant collects his wits, fear of separation is his first fear, followed around six months of age by fear of sudden noises and the loss of support. Throughout their lives, human beings are startled most of all by abruptness. A loud noise that begins softly and builds to its volume will not disturb a baby, but he will scream in terror if a newspaper unexpectedly is crackled near his ear. Similarly, adults retreat from a friendship offered too quickly, find the quick transitions of jet travel a trial and are immobile for an instant at even trivial mishaps they didn't forsee. In the first two years, toddlers develop other fears: loud noises and objects associated with noise, strangers, new situations. They are *not* afraid of darkness, slimy or furry animals or horror masks.

Researchers asked fifty-one children and ninety adults to handle a selection of snakes. In all the age groups, only the two-year-olds were relaxed and curious. The three-year-olds showed a degree of caution, while the four-year-olds were definitely apprehensive. Those most upset by the experiment were the ninety adults.

Concrete fears, such as a fear of horses or frogs, begin to disappear as the child grows; if they remain into adolescence, chances are that they are permanent. A young child apparently can be conditioned out of a fear almost as easily as it was planted. Some time after Dr. Watson's coldhearted experiments on Albert, researchers discovered another child whose fears were identical to those conditioned in Albert. The little boy, then two, was terrified of all furry animals and even recoiled from a ball of wool. Rabbits frightened him most, so the psychologists put a rabbit near him while he ate food that he liked and invited three other children, who adored rabbits, to play with the little boy while the rabbit was loose in the room. The unconditioning began with the child shrieking even when he saw the rabbit in a cage and ended four months later with the little boy chuckling while the rabbit nibbled his fingers.

Major fears of young children concern imaginary dangers, storms, the supernatural, war, destruction and death. The fear of inadequacy, which most people never overcome, begins around the age of nine. Adolescents mostly are afraid of ridicule and of being unpopular, though adolescent girls may demonstrate showy panic over snakes or high places. Adults have fears about sex, or authority; they dread failure and may be appalled at success; they carry a heavy load of social fears, which psychoanalyst Karen Horney explains as stemming from a misplaced center of gravity—one based on the opinion and good will of others, rather than on self-esteem. Such dependence on admiration from strangers, friends and relatives leaves the personality perpetually imperiled.

Up until the age of four, all human beings are instantly responsive to suggestions of danger. After that age, naïveté gives way to a more sophisticated judgment. Among the most fear-instilling experiences during the vulnerable period are confinement, particularly in darkness, desertion in a strange place and witnessing coitus. The latter may be associated in a child's mind with a life-and-death struggle, very sinister and cruel. It can leave in its wake fear of the dark, distaste for physical contact of every kind and a revulsion for sexual relationships.

Men suppress their fears more than women, but have as many. While a woman will refuse flatly to stand on the edge of a parapet, a man does so nonchalantly but feels relieved when he steps back.

Psychoanalyst Otto Rank postulated two major fears: one a death fear and the other a life fear. The life fear is the terror of being separated from protection, beginning, he thought, with an infant's reluctant parting from the womb. This is the more destructive fear, since it chains the personality to helplessness and loss of individuality as a technique of avoiding independence. The death fear, on the other hand, stimulates people to live more acutely. They are pressed to make a vital effort to develop themselves in defiance of all forms of stagnation and death. All persons, Rank believed, are ruled by one or the other fear; the tone of their life style is either a retreat from the commitments of living or a sally against the inertia of death.

Many people invent their own fears, rather than tolerate the floating fearfulness they cannot understand. They seize on fads—lung cancer, radiation and insanity have devoted followings—and channel their fear in that direction. In a simpler age, fearful people drew comfort from being afraid of the elements or heavenly portents. It is vastly more re-assuring to have a label for a state of fear than to cope with the horror of abstract dread. Fear is somehow relieved by finding an acceptable target, so most people are prudent enough to select one that won't be considered absurd by their friends.

A man who was depressed on the morning he was making a long plane trip devised a fear of airplane travel to explain his mood, and subsequently enlarged his fear until he was physically ill before every flight. A housewife with only a modest level of fear to dispose of imagined a fear of heights. The idea came to her while carrying her infant son down some stairs and two days later she was nervous on a ladder.

It's fool's work to try to cure someone of the comfort of his pet fear. If logic prevails and the fear is detached from its convenient object, the hapless person must find a new and less vulnerable fear. One young man had fastened his fears on the conviction that he would die of a ruptured appendix. He pleaded with a surgeon to remove his healthy appendix, and simultaneously his fear, but the doctor refused. "If I take out your appendix," he explained, "you'll only switch to being afraid of something else, like cancer. A rup-tured appendix fear is much easier to deal with, believe me." The man was impressed. Ever since, he has been untroubled by his appendix phobia, but he is tortured by his dread of cancer.

Studies of fearful people have shown that many of them received scant evidence in their early years that the world is a safe and friendly place. They were harshly and abruptly punished and grew up in wretched anticipation of injustice and rejection. Baby Albert was conditioned to a simple fear, furriness, in one week, but the deconditioning process re-quired four months. Apparently years and years of relaxed, reliable friendships and home environment would be needed to cure someone deeply frightened.

Overprotected children suffer the same fate as roughly

treated ones, since coddling robs them of confidence in themselves and opportunity to develop their resources. Sadly, many adults with over- or underprivileged backgrounds are beyond the salvation of good luck and achievement. They are apt to be suspicious of success, doubting strongly that it will last.

Children granted independence and raised with warmth and affection generally have only routine fears which are easily outgrown. Psychologists have noted that they can survive savagery, such as being sexually molested, without detectable psychic harm. Being strangers to early betrayal, they trust the future and can tolerate the occasional catastrophe.

Curiously, a point of difference between fearful and confident adults is the manner in which they describe their parents. Both may declare love and respect, but those whom psychologists have identified as highly afraid always give physical descriptions of their mothers and fathers and a list of the material benefits provided by them. They speak glowingly of the stern discipline, which they profess to admire for its fairness and intractability. The most vivid fear they can recall is the fear of being punished.

On the other hand, people with a low fear content will describe their parents in terms of their emotional quality, how they felt about one another, what kindness and consideration they demonstrated to their family. Their recollections of early fears are the ordinary childhood ones.

Fear has two extremes, the blush of shyness which nature intends as a rosy concealment and the stampede of panic, which is instant madness.

Shyness occurs, most frequently in young people, when the situation seems more difficult than the ego is prepared to handle. Experience and confidence gained from the repetition of social ordeals eventually relieves the fluster and helplessness.

But everyone is susceptible to panic. Dr. Meerloo writes, "Panic is a contagious flight reflex." Panic is total loss of control. Women have trampled their own children and men have bolted from burning houses, leaving their families behind. The only effective means of dealing with panic is to prevent it, in the hush that instantly descends when a shocking danger is perceived. Unhappily, no one knows himself well enough to predict whether he will leap to his feet to take superb command of the evacuation or whether he will blindly lead the rush for the doors. "A panicky person," observes Dr. Meerloo, "causes more fear than the danger itself."

A psychologist who has spent years studying human reactions in crisis periods was aboard a DC-8 that crashed at Idlewild (now Kennedy) Airport in 1960 during a blizzard. Trained as he was, he remembers little of what happened. Someone else opened an escape door, called out calmly, "This way please," and led the ninety-eight passengers to safety. When he collected himself, the psychologist was in a position to state authoritatively, "In most cases of crowd panic in a confined area, fear of not being able to escape is the cause of virtually all terror."

Some believe that fear is fundamentally not knowing what to do. People have little fear within the area of their capabilities. Yale University made two interesting studies to illustrate the value of preparation in reducing fear. The first concerned a group of high school students, half of whom were instructed on the progress Russia was making toward building its own A-bomb. Three months later, President Harry Truman announced that the Soviet had just tested an A-bomb. The students who had been alerted to this possibility were noticeably less concerned than those who were surprised.

The other study involved men undergoing surgery. Three groups were discovered to be highly agitated. One was comprised of men who made their alarm obvious and the other of men who were concealing their distress under arrogance. Neither group wanted details of the operations and both were highly disturbed and angry during the discomfort of the postoperative period. A third group, men who were apprehensive and demanded full explanations of procedures and what miseries they might expect, was composed and unruffled both before and after the operations.

One young mother reported that her nearly-three-year-old persisted in playing near a steep embankment. She warned him that if he slipped over the edge, she wouldn't hear him call and it would take a long time before she found him. One morning he disappeared and she searched his usual haunts for half an hour before remembering the embankment. She found him there, clinging to a bush halfway down, tranquil and unafraid. He had expected to wait awhile to be rescued, so the delay didn't trouble him at all.

The multiple fears of children have been ascribed to the impossibility of preparing them for a world that will startle and be strange. Their smallness and lack of physical skills cause them to feel vulnerable and pitifully frail. Until they develop a few accomplishments, beginning with the securing of their parents' affection, they cannot be brave at all.

Fearful adults similarly feel that the world is too difficult and too threatening. The prevalence of unhealthy fear in the world today is a fuse than can wipe out the human race. Rather than bear their alarm that war may begin unexpectedly, many people are in a mood to lob the first missile. Decency and compassion are obliterated by fear; those who are frightened would see the world destroyed, so long as they are spared. Judgment becomes incoherent hate. A madman, promising any kind of safety at any price, can impress a country driven to selfishness by fear.

Prejudice is one of the commonest faces of fear. Dreading their fellow man because they feel inadequate, fearful people become adamantly bigoted. Citizens want to close their ranks against strangers, and therefore feel betrayed by reasonable men who talk of democratic ideals. It has been noted that those whose basic fears are sexual turn on Negroes, believing them superior in this regard, and those whose basic fear is economic failure turn on the Jewish. They cry for more restrictions, more repression, more red tape, more police, more violence. It is all the sound that fear makes.

In contrast, fear has magnificent consequences. Philosophers from Statius to Santayana have declared that it was fear that led to the invention of the gods—and religion when interpreted lovingly is an ennobling force in the world. Milton believed that hope cannot exist without fear. "We could not be stirred by the possibility of success," wrote psychologist Frederick H. Lund, "if there was no possibility of defeat." Antoine de Saint-Exupéry observed that when danger comes men "discover that they belong to the same family." Many scientists believe that the record of human achievement is the record of men who were afraid of being insignificant.

The most valiant act of which moral fiber is capable is the deliberate overcoming of fear. In *We Are Not Afraid*, Maurice Duhamel notes, "A man is stronger morally, and physically too very often, for he has been able to find strength he did not know he possessed . . . his fibre has been toughened, his soul firmed, his muscles flexed, his mind sharpened."

Fear that is not vanquished, brooding, hating, dark fear, is eternally destructive. Seneca wrote wisely, two thousand years ago, "Nothing is terrible in things, except fear itself."

CHAPTER FOUR

Most Courage Is a Fake

Courage is the quality men admire most, though they rarely recognize it in themselves. Primitive males measured their manhood by it, and so do modern adolescents up to the age of Hemingway. Civilized, circumscribed people are dazzled by showy courage: the Mexican who dives off a cliff into an ebbing sea, racing car drivers with chiseled faces, blur-bodied trapeze artists and the bystanders who run through flames to save strangers.

Some of this kind of heroism really stems from the scruffy element in human nature. Hatred, for instance, can produce suicidal courage, guilt can look like dedication, envy nerves a man for spectacular effort, loneliness makes him rakish, anger underlies a good deal of slashing valor and the fear of humiliation, retaliation or exposure often wears a look of fearlessness.

There is a truer courage, more gallant and practically invisible, in the steadfastness of ordinary people in monotonous jobs, in parents who matter-of-factly raise handicapped children, in those who live in never ending pain without hating the well, in unloved adults who stalwartly give up malice and suspicion and teach themselves to relax and trust.

There is also the highest form of courage: moral courage. It is an asset which makes a man indestructible.

Much of what appears to the world as courageous is actually preparation and familiarity. Ski jumpers, big-game hunters and astronauts are unconcerned because of years spent in training and practice. In an emergency, their relaxed brains provide them with workable choices, while the intelligence of the novice is locked in a paralysis of terror. A woman who had a collection of venomous snakes was bitten in the arm by a king cobra and calmly called the hospital, directing first aid treatment until the ambulance arrived. Her control stemmed from her lifelong familiarity with snakebite procedure, but when she later died she was described as a heroine.

Similarly, the courage of a seasoned soldier is a compound in which experience is the looming factor. His pitiless occupation in wartime becomes bearable if he learns to pamper his weapons, sort out which battle noises are dangerous, locate good cover, tolerate the betrayals of his viscera and dreams and strengthen himself with the pride of being able to function well.

Few men consider themselves brave, maybe none. Everyday use takes the luster out of even bullfighting, sky-diving, mountain climbing. There are always what seem more valiant men, who took more risks, operated under greater handicaps, dared more gaudily.

A Canadian veterans' hospital had a patient for many years who became a legend because of the pain he had endured. A sniper's bullet in Korea had smashed his hip and sent a hundred splinters of bone through his body. When his dressings were changed, he bent steel rods in his hands and screamed. Later he insisted that he was better off than the amputees. The amputees, however, considered themselves luckier than the blind and the blind felt sorry for the paraplegics. The paraplegics didn't regard themselves as courageous—the really brave man was the one who was dying quietly of kidney cancer. But that patient was convinced he would recover.

Among the kinds of courage is group courage, a contagion spread by some remarkable leader or by a group standard. Six Nation Indians walk the steel beams of skyscraper skeletons because the job fulfills all the conditions of a victorious war party: it is awesome and well belted with the scalps of timid, and therefore inferior, whites. The Royal Navy, Highland regiments, *Panzer* divisions, kamikaze pilots and marines stand steady because they are convinced they can. When cities are besieged, the populations usually exult in the jaunty sensation of shared superiority over hardship.

Some leaders, generally men whom psychologists would describe as "father figures," have a hypnotic power to transport their followers into demi-madness beyond their own strength, ability or judgment. Julius Caesar was such a leader. Plutarch describes how his devoted soldiers fought: one had his right arm severed by a sword but fought on with his left and captured a ship; another had an eye put out by an arrow, his shoulder and thigh pierced by javelins and one hundred and thirty darts in his shield, but he continued to fight. In 1917, a Dutch general soundly scolded his terrified troops, put a cigar between his teeth, lifted his saber and led them into an attack.

Some heroism is helped by an idealized vision of the self. Many of history's most fearless leaders were raving paranoics; modern psychiatry would certify insane Alexander, Joan of Arc and Napoleon, to name a few of the most illustrious. The vitality of their vision was irresistible to their followers, but their bravery was mostly egocentricity.

The same necessity to be superlative operates in lesser-known men. A man who thinks of himself as a great benefactor must choose between risking his life to save a drowning child or else having to give up the delusion. Adults with theories of infallibility are compelled to stick to their posts until they die. Teen-agers with nothing to buffer their self-doubts but a show of boldness will be unable to avoid a test of car courage.

The results of such nervous bravery are often appalling. Adults have leaped into rivers to rescue the drowning, only to remember too late that they themselves cannot swim. Nobly self-sacrificing men have pushed adrift lifeboats containing only women and children, who subsequently perish through lack of sea knowledge. Clerks have had their heads blown off fussily protecting the petty cash.

A great deal of courage is rooted in self-hatred. Harry Houdini, the escape artist, thrilled millions with his daring, but Louis J. Bragman later wrote in the *Psychoanalytic Review*, "almost every stunt staged by Houdini represented a form of pseudo-suicide."

People in pathetic pursuit of a feeling of worth perform an incalculable volume of courageous acts, which encompass almost all the unnecessary braveries of young men, since the dramatic aggressiveness of heroism suits the male spirit. They risk death to seek a talisman of fate: if they survive the tilt, it is an omen that they have value. The reward is a flash of self-liking, a swell of glory that Antoine de Saint-Exupéry called the birth of the sleeping prince within every man. If they don't survive, who cares; they weren't enjoying life very much anyway.

The United States psychoanalyst-writer, Erich Fromm, terms this kind of risk-taking, "the courage of nihilism, a willingness to throw life away because one is incapable of loving it." D. H. Munro, a New Zealand philosopher, has commented, "Strenuous heroism is often, in practice, a synonym for ruthless bigotry."

Some men never advance beyond their compulsion for defiant living. Middle-aged and potbellied with drink, they handle the controls of their airplanes carelessly, contemptuously stride into the jungle, keep a collection of guns.

It is true to a moderate degree of Winston Churchill, who in his youth in Egypt managed to take part in one of the

world's last cavalry charges and who, when Britian desperately needed him, heartily detested taking elementary precautions against being killed.

It is more true of the late Briton, Lieutenant-General Sir
Adrian Carton de Wiart, who was wounded eleven times in
various wars. His left hand was shot off in 1915 at Ypres but
he continued to lead an attack, pulling the pins out of grenades
with his teeth. "I was thankful my teeth were my own," he
commented cheerily. When he lost an eye in Somaliland, he
was delighted. "Thank God," he chortled. "This will take me
out of this tinpot show to the real battle in France." In peacetime he liked pigsticking and dueling with cobras.

It is true most of all of Ernest Hemingway, the most
celebrated courage-lover of modern times. He described courage as "grace under pressure" and when he wasn't putting
himself to brinkmanship tests, he was watching others do it—
bullfighters, hunters, demented generals. Gaudy courage isn't
considered an indication of an abundance of character and
moral sinew, but of a deficit. It is a pathetic device to overcome numbness and self-intolerance.

Jean Anouilh has an observation in his play *Becket*. During
a wild-boar hunt, the King asks Thomas à Becket why he
seems to crave danger. Becket replies gaily, "One has to
gamble with one's life to feel alive."

The courting of danger is also an effective antidote for
anxiety. There is very little neurosis, for instance, in a population that is being bombed. Floating, crawling fears that
fester both mind and digestion will welcome a definite,
genuine, certified menace. There is a paradoxical sense of
buoyant relief under the guns. Many adults, accordingly, become addicted to jeopardy—it is the drug which keeps them
from fragmenting into a breakdown. By clinging to a high-
risk profession or recreation, one capable of either killing or
maiming them, they can experience exhilaration even in
peacetime.

"People often prefer fearful reality to fearful fantasy," the
Dutch psychiatrist A. M. Meerloo has written. "The auda-

cious deeds of the Partisans were not always courage, but the dangerous wish to end insecure tension."

There is also the courage of dull-wittedness. Peasant armies that tramped stolidly through thousands of years of carnage, blinking in the sun at Antioch, Hastings and Waterloo, were composed mainly of unimaginative men. "Yokel soldiers, with the courage of a vacant mind," they are dismissed by a British doctor, Lord Moran, who wrote *The Anatomy of Courage* after spending from 1914 to 1917 in the trenches and part of the next war tending R.A.F. pilots.

"They drew no pictures of danger for their own undoing," he says of all militia previous to this century. "Phlegm, that was the yokel's virtue as a soldier; it was the distinctive quality of his race." He adds, "Men suffered more in the last war [1914–1918], as it seems to me, not because it was more terrible but because they were more sensitive."

Today's sensitive man, however, can be reduced to the state of a dazed simpleton when his brain cannot tolerate any more noise, horror and pain. A Spitfire pilot in the Battle of Britain recalls the action for which he received a Distinguished Flying Cross. He had been in a prolonged dogfight over London and was in an advanced stage of exhaustion when a German bomber crossed his sights. He bore down on it automatically, until he ran out of ammunition, at which point it seemed to him eminently sensible to continue on and ram the enemy. "It was either very childish of me, or insane," he explains. "It was not brave, not in the least. It just never occurred to me that my aircraft would even be damaged."

Dr. Meerloo relates how a Dutch soldier became a hero. Planes and ground forces had been attacking his part of the line and a retreat was ordered. This soldier was too frightened to move. He remained at his position, firing hysterically. The enemy unexpectedly panicked and fled and he was decorated for valorous conduct.

A Canadian, Brigadier Dollard Ménard, who charged a pillbox on the Dieppe beach although he had been wounded four times, later dissected his emotions during the one-man attack. They had four elements, he said, none of them courage: first was egoism, optimism or thoughtlessness; next, discipline; third, anger, because a good friend had been shot in the stomach; finally, he didn't give a damn.

Discipline and instinct seem to be prime instigators of many acts of courage. Normal people have a reflexive tendency to protect life put in their charge. The golfer Ben Hogan, for example, had no time to form a conscious thought when a bus skidded in front of his car in 1949, but he instantly flung his body in front of his wife. She escaped with scratches but he had bones broken from his collarbone to his ankle.

A young grandmother picnicking with her two-year-old granddaughter near Toronto one summer afternoon snatched the child out of the way of horses bolting toward them with a heavy wagon. The child was safe, but iron wheels passed over the woman's body and crippled her for life.

In wartime, countless officers and non-commissioned officers have tried to lob away grenades from which green soldiers inadvertently have pulled the pins. Some were blinded, some lost their right hands, a few got away with it. When a training balloon burst over England in 1962, the instructor realized that one student in the gondola was too terrified to use his parachute. He stayed with him and, as they neared the ground, shouted in a parade-ground voice, "Brace yourself and lift your feet." They walked away with minor injuries.

Andrew Carnegie took note of this responsible kind of courage, which he felt was triggered not by character but by the hero's clear duty. He therefore set up his unique Carnegie Hero Fund Commission to reward the brave who are neither police, firemen, soldiers, relatives or others in positions of authority. He established the fund in 1904 with five million dollars worth of U. S. Steel bonds. It has since given away more than nine million dollars to heroes or the next of kin of deceased heroes. The annual list of citations is a moving testimonial to the brotherhood and nobility inherent in what is known as the ordinary man.

It catalogues a succession of men, women and children diving in front of falling objects to protect strangers, descending into pits filled with lethal gas to rescue the unconscious, rushing into burning buildings and treacherous water. A Silver Medal and one thousand dollars went to a New York waiter, for example, who climbed four floors in a tenement building that was collapsing under and over him and carried out an eighty-three-year-old woman. A young girl swam to the aid of a man being devoured by a shark and towed him to shore while the shark continued to attack. She received a Silver Medal and seven hundred and fifty dollars.

A man who lost his left arm as he chose to crash his disabled gravel truck into a tree rather than chance hitting a school bus was given a Bronze Medal and a thousand dollars. The last individual Gold Medal, together with a life pension, went in 1924 to the widow of a man who walked into a small house that literally was filled with fire, flames licking through every crack and window, and succeeded in saving one of the two small children inside. Gold Medals, mounted on bronze tablets, have been presented twice to groups: in memory of the *Titanic* passengers and crew in 1912 and to the survivors of the Springhill mine disaster in Nova Scotia in 1958.

Throughout the history of man, a few have somehow summoned up a private resource that propels them into filthy, horrible tasks they could have sidestepped without blame. Fate puts them in the way of agony, and they decide to endure it. Jackie Robinson, the Negro baseball star who withstood scalding vilification when he was the first of his race to play in the major leagues, once expressed this brand of courage eloquently: "It's being able to rise up, I guess, when you have to."

It turns up all over the globe, in baroque forms. In 1962, a swagger-sticked British major was assigned to a Nigerian unit of the United Nations forces in the Congo. Informed that the Congolese had massacred twenty priests, leaving one alive, he calmly set off unarmed to rescue the survivor. When he emerged from his aircraft, he was surrounded by eight hundred half-naked Congolese. He approached them briskly, shook hands with the largest, gathered up the priest and departed.

During the Boxer Rebellion, a timid Boston missionary, Mary Morrill, stepped outside the compound wall, faced a howling mob and asked them to spare the other inhabitants, killing her instead if they wanted a life. They dispersed in astonishment, but returned the next day to slaughter the colony and behead her.

Fear is a form of energy that generates itself spontaneously in every human emergency. For this reason, the courage of control is a dam against emotional release, and must eventually give way if the health and sanity of the individual are to be preserved. The mother who under tight control gets her battered child to the hospital afterwards may faint, have hysterics or go into shock. Sailors off wartime convoys had foul tempers, displayed an animal cruelty in their humor and relished brutal barroom fights. Soldiers who crouch stolidly under bombardment for long periods, such as occurred during trench warfare in the First World War, never entirely recover. For the rest of their lives, certain sounds—sometimes only the wind in the trees—will make them shudder.

The Royal Navy has a famous hero, a captain who sipped tea on the bridge of his ship while a lookout gave him bulletins on an approaching dive-bomber. Not until the lookout reported, "Bomb released, sir," did the captain turn his head and in a normal tone of voice order, "Hard a-starboard." While the bomb exploded harmlessly a few yards away, he took another sip of tea. But when the raid was over, he went down into his cabin where he could be alone and wept.

Long-term courage, therefore, is truly superhuman. Medgar Evers, National Association for the Advancement of Colored People official who lived in a small Mississippi community during nine years of unrelenting harassment in order to organize Negroes to register for voting, is such a figure.

Eventually he died with an assassin's bullet in his back. James H. Meredith, the first known Negro to attend the University of Mississippi, is another example. A British newspaper, *The Observer*, suggested that Meredith be granted a World Medal for heroism, for daring to "incarnate in his own person humanity's struggle against racial oppression and mob fanaticism."

Similarly, the poor in health sometimes live courageously, year in and year out, refusing to allow weakness, nausea or pain deter them from making their existence count for something. Herbert Spencer, the English philosopher who founded philosophy, had a general nervous breakdown that destroyed his health when he was thirty-five. Nevertheless, he commenced his eighteen-volume *Synthetic Philosophy* the first year of his illness. The pains in his head were so severe that he had to dose himself with opium in order to sleep at night. Finally he could dictate only ten minutes at a time, five times a day. He wrote *Principles of Sociology* that way.

Charles Darwin was so ill after he returned from his voyage on the *Beagle* that he never again was able to work more than a few hours a day. He completed the bulk of his life work under those conditions. Robert Louis Stevenson wrote incessantly while dying of tuberculosis. A Toronto physician who is the mother of three children discovered in 1959 that she was a victim of multiple sclerosis. Though her right arm and leg became almost useless, she took a part-time job as a school medical examiner and in the summer operated a girls' camp She was inspired, she said, by a line her mother wrote in the family Bible when she was dying of cancer. "I practice the heroism of carrying on."

The suffering that human beings can bear strains credulity. If he wills it, a man can withstand torture, disease, grief, poverty, cold, boredom, isolation, failure and the caprice of his fellow man. Marcus Aurelius conceived the theory that "nothing happens to any man which he is not formed by nature to bear."

When a man is determined to submit himself to danger,

nature is helpful. He gets extra adrenalin to give him abnormal strength and endurance. The pituitary gland—the "gland of courage"—secretes some magic. (Experiments in removing pituitary glands from animals produced four-legged cowards.) There is also a degree of hypalgesia, immunity to pain. This is called the blinkers effect. In the outmost extremity of fighting fear, men cannot feel wounds or fractures and a daze descends on their imaginations. They experience a dreamy detachment in the midst of struggle and terror.

Everyday heroism is not accompanied by drama. The psychoanalyst Alfred Adler once listed three areas in a normal life which demand courage to be well met: social relations, occupation and marriage. There is majesty but no showiness in a man who gamely meets his responsibilities, holds himself together despite boredom, mortification or turmoil and believes in fairness.

"Our banal everyday life makes banal demands on our patience, our devotedness, endurance, self-sacrifice and so on," wrote philosopher-psychoanalyst Carl G. Jung, "which we must fulfill modestly and without any heroic gestures to court applause, and which actually need a heroism which is not seen from without. It does not shine and is not praised . . ."

Invisible courage is part of all growth. Giving up a long-held conviction or grudge is like an amputation; there is consequent pain and doubt that the new attitude will prove as comfortable and serviceable as the old. To go on, humans must valiantly keep shedding themselves. Some people can move agilely to absorb new information and points of view, but for others advancement is scary.

"Each step forward is a step into the unfamiliar and is possibly dangerous," comments Abraham Maslow, president of the Brandeis University department of psychology. "It also means giving up something familiar and good and satisfying. It frequently means a parting and a separation, even a kind of death prior to a rebirth, with consequent nostalgia, fear, loneliness and mourning. It also often means giving up a simpler and easier and less effortful life in exchange for a more demanding, more responsible, more difficult life.

"Growth forward is in spite of these losses and therefore requires courage, will choice and strength in the individual, as well as protection, permission and encouragement from the environment, especially for the child."

A theologian, Professor Paul Tillich of Union Theological Seminary, has declared that courage means "the acceptance of want, toil, insecurity, pain, possible destruction. Without this self-affirmation, life could not be preserved or increased."

Courage is so private that a prizefighter may have none of it, being bonded instead of coarse opportunity, good reflexes and lust for revenge, while a man who apologizes to his son may have waded through crocodiles.

Admiral Bull Halsey made a famous comment on heroes. "There are no great men," he stated, "only great challenges ordinary men are asked to face." Few great challenges crackle with the unmistakable drum-roll of destiny. Inconspicuously, courage makes a daily triumph over misery, death, frustration and injustice—in wretched homes, kept spotless and planted with geraniums, in the daring vitality of some old people, in gentle poets who lay railway ties for a living and send their sons to college, in ministers who denounce their congregations for excluding a Jew from a country club dance.

Men who resolutely step into the path of a great challenge sometimes catch a hold on history. The Irishman Edmund Burke, freshly elected to represent prosperous and insular Bristol in the House of Commons two hundred years ago, coined an ethic when he informed his constituents that he had no intention of following all their instructions. A man's "unbiased opinion, his mature judgment, his enlightened conscience, he ought not to sacrifice to you, to any man, or to any set of men living. These he does not derive from your pleasure, they are a trust from providence." At the first opportunity, Bristol turned him out.

George Washington, a wealthy aristocrat inclined to the fastidious avoidance of unpleasantness, spent six thankless years as the head of a sometimes barefoot, usually hungry, frequently cowardly, reluctant and thieving rabble, without the support—financial or moral—of his own Congress. Once he was virtually without ammunition for six months and he constantly was beset by intrigue to have him removed. He sighed mildly, "I could wish that the dispute had been left to posterity to determine," but stuck it.

Thomas Paine, in a period that tolerated no religious doubt whatsoever, wrote *The Age of Reason*, in which he asserted "My own mind is my own church." Amidst threats to lynch him, he circulated the pamphlet himself. Abraham Lincoln fought the extremists of both the North and the South, searching for a compromise that would avert civil war. For his trouble, he was cursed by both sides. Henry David Thoreau, noting that his country still supported slavery, had entered into a shameful war with Mexico and mistreated its Indian population, urged his fellow citizens to stop paying taxes and went to prison. He said prison was the only true place for a just man anyway.

The NAACP chairman in Virginia, Rev. Francis Griffin, paraphrased Thoreau in September 1963, at the close of a summer of bitterness. "In this country," he informed his congregation, "there are plenty of things worth going to jail for."

Often men can't choose their challenge—they are chosen by it. A United States soldier, Harold Russell, awakened in a hospital bed to discover that both his hands had been amputated. He later wrote, "In one way or another, each of us must pass through the fires at least once in his lifetime. Each of us must find out for himself that his handicaps, his failures and shortcomings must be conquered or else he must perish. It is not what you have lost, but what you have left that counts."

Socrates once complained that "we have failed to discover what courage is," a curious declaration from a man who possessed so much of it. Philosophers, including the slyly ingenuous Socrates, have always defined courage by a man's interior finery, which may never show, rather than by the handful of splendid sorties into danger or unpopularity that he records.

Courage, they say, is the decision to wear one's real personality instead of a contrivance deemed admirable by the neighbors. It is the mark of those who unfurl their best flags, risking derision.

Courage is the ability to love wholeheartedly, without seeking the safeguard of power over the loved one or the gluey tactic of dependency. It is also the ability to be loved, without squirming with unworthiness and skepticism. Courage makes living a personal creation, rather than a mass-produced gadget festooned with definitions, directions for use and assurances that it won't hurt.

Courage is such faith in self, in the purpose and dignity of all life, that it becomes a cathedral. Courage is so perceptive that it marks and fights an injustice even though it belongs to a tradition and has acceptance; it recognizes a charlatan, no matter how distinguished his robes.

Courage is the sense to be idle in a world which is annoyed at inactivity. Gandhi took one day off every week for silence and prayer, to restore his mental freshness and save himself from "becoming formal, mechanical and devitalised." Men and women of courage put emptiness into their routine—in order to listen to clouds and greet their souls.

Courage is so stalwart it doesn't need to be perfect. Courage doesn't mind dying because it is living so well.

There is a momentum to courage. No act of courage is an island. Each one adds to a man's hope for himself and advances his confidence in his goodness, his integrity and his faith. Since these are the heart of courage, he is enlarging by each brave act his ability to be brave. Eventually the process is irreversible.

Judge Learned Hand, son and grandson of judges and a venerated U.S. circuit court judge, once observed, "Man's highest courage is to bet his all on what is no more than the best guess he can make, ask no warranties and distrust all such; face the puzzle of life without any kit of ready-made answers . . ."

Cicero said, "Whoever is brave is a man of great soul." Gary Cooper, the movie star who died as well as a man can, echoed him: "Courage or guts originate in the true heart of the machinery, which is the mind."

Real courage, like real love and maturity, is not common. Lord Moran noted sadly, "The honor of our race is in the keeping of but a fraction of her people."

Some days, it is enough.

CHAPTER FIVE

Bottled Anger Can Kill You

Anger, mankind's most primitive emotion, is also the most obvious one. While the more disabling emotions of hate, fear and loneliness can be masked, few people can hide anger. It's noisy, humiliating, destructive and ubiquitous—so much so that one specialist in animal behavior seriously insists that man is only a quarrelsome species of ape, the missing link between anthropoids and true human beings.

When people speak of controlling their emotions, they generally mean their tempers. Between bouts of anger, men and women have more regrets about their own waspishness than about any other aspect of their personalities. They sourly view the paradox of anger: psychiatry considers it unhealthy to repress a rage, but experience demonstrates that any other course will result in remorse and reprisals.

One of the most appalling discoveries a person can make about himself is to meet the hellhound of anger he contains. A glimpse of this inner hyena leaves a man shaken and confused; he is a long time convincing his ego that he is really a civilized and harmless being.

This is not surprising, since anger is the least civilized attribute of man. It springs from the oldest and deepest part of the brain, a small clump of lunatic cells that hasn't changed much in ten million years. Dwarfed under the huge mass of the cerebrum, the large brain mass that evolved over the centuries to enable man to reason and be kind, the tiny caveman brain seems comparatively insignificant. But when surgery or an injury—including an injury to self-esteem—disturbs the thinking processes, the primeval fury can leap free.

The phenomenon has been observed repeatedly in hospitals and laboratories. Brain damage in mild, pleasant people can transform them into vicious psychopaths. Electrodes placed against the hypothalamus of cats can induce instant rage at the flick of a switch. Harvard University's physiologist Walter B. Cannon was intrigued many years ago to discover that "rapid removal of the cerebral hemispheres was followed by an extraordinary exhibition of rage." Others have observed that the last emotion left in a paralyzed brain is wild, strong anger.

When normal people are in a state of extreme anger, the rest of the brain is as impotent as if it had been paralyzed. Outlandish courses of action seem reasonable and even urgent. The imagination becomes so full of schemes for revenge and destruction that humanity is wiped away. Alcohol is almost as effective as surgery in taking out wisdom; by dulling the cerebral man, it loosens the control of anger.

Some human behavior experts believe that man is born in an angry mood. An infant's first cry, they claim, is one of wrath at the discomfort of his birth. Karl Menninger, a distinguished U.S. psychiatrist, has written, "The human child begins his life in anger." Most authorities, however, don't agree, believing that the brain of a newborn is too muddled to produce a distinct emotion until he is a few months old. He feels distress only, a compound of three reactions—fear because he is helpless, anger at the world which dominates him and hatred of the mother who only intermittently helps him.

Studies of adult anger illustrate that grown men and women lose their tempers for much the same basic reason as babies do, because of some loss of a sense of invincibility. Anger is the reflexive reaction to any blow that damages inner prestige. Conversely, nothing renders people more impervious to anger than a mood of self-approval and confidence.

Jean-Paul Sartre is impressed with the theory of anger that it is the expression of a defeat. When people fail to solve their problems, they tend to fall back on this primitive nervous circuit. He notes that two friends can exchange banter in high humor, so long as the insults are even; when one man begins to run out of material, he then begins to grow angry. Temper is a universal technique for dealing with humiliation.

The angriest people in the world normally are the two-year-olds. Beset by their smallness and by admonishing adults, two-year-olds are almost continuously frustrated and furious. One researcher easily compiled a list of one hundred sure causes of anger in this age group, but other estimates run into the thousands. Even one-year-olds are pretty ferocious.

"Children between the ages of one and two, when put together in a playpen, will bite each other, pull each other's hair and steal each other's toys," noted Anna Freud, who worked in nurseries in wartime London. "The more their independence and strength are growing, the more they will have to be watched."

Florence L. Goodenough, professor at the University of Minnesota's Institute of Child Study, published a much respected study, *Anger in Young Children*. She observed three styles of displaying anger when, for instance, a pull toy is stuck behind the leg of a chair. One method is what Dr. Goodenough calls undirected anger—the child just stands and screams. Another is to offer resistance, by pulling frantically at the toy. The third is retaliation, where the child kicks the chair or tries to break the toy.

As the child grows older, retaliation becomes a more and more favored method of expressing anger, particularly in boys. It takes some odd, spiteful forms: mussing freshly brushed hair or prolonging thumb-sucking because it annoys mother. Three-year-olds are beginning to be social beings, which results in tantrums over the behavior of other children. All preschool children are touchiest when hungry or sleepy, when there are visitors in the home (particularly child guests), when they are ill. Routine makes them seethe, all of it—bedtime, mealtime, washing, putting toys away.

Dr. William E. Blatz, founder of the University of Toronto's Institute of Child Study, reported that retaliatory fighting reaches its peak during the first year of school, drops off at the age of seven and has almost disappeared in the early teens. Adolescents demonstrate anger by being sulky and impertinent.

The taming of a child's temper, in fact, is a steady process of driving it underground rather than removing it. Little children, like apes and the insane, put on a fireworks display of anger that lasts only a minute or two, after which cheerfulness is restored with bewildering suddenness. Adults require themselves to control a show of anger and as a result steam more or less visibly for ten to twenty minutes, after which they are grumpy for hours or even days.

Like children, adults are most irritable just before a meal or when they are ill or tired. Surprisingly, holidays and weekends are periods of increased testiness. Psychiatrists say that only very stable, mature persons can tolerate the freedom of leisure without being disturbed and unsure.

The level of irritability varies so strikingly from one person to another that it poses an absorbing problem for the scientists. Some postulate that very angry, tense people were born to mothers who were taut and upset during their pregnancies. Such infants, they believe, begin life in a hostile mood and steadily grow more belligerent because their tempers create rejection and disapproval, which in turn nourishes the growth of anger.

Bottle-fed babies, according to some psychiatrists, are more likely to feel mistreated than breast-fed babies and therefore may become easily provoked adults. Younger children in a family generally exhibit more anger than first-borns, a repressed crew who turn their anger inward and suffer from depression. Early illness seems to be critical in the development of anger capacity. One study found that adults who were sickly, especially before the age of six, seemed to have established a permanent pattern of being easily affronted.

The most important determining factor, though, is the personality of the mother. The anger in infants is always directed against the woman-made environment of their nurseries. If the mother, or mother-substitute, is punitive, indifferent or callous, the baby is in a steady state of dismay and indignation. Similarly, if the mother is intrusively solicitous and hovers over her child, his development and independence are hampered, which also makes him exceedingly angry. The emotional tone of a young child whose circumstances keep him testy can solidify and result in an adult with a trigger temper.

In *The Fears Men Live By*, Selma G. Hirsh comments, "It was startling to see how often the anger expressed by the prejudiced adult turned out to be nearly as old as he was himself."

Angry adults, as psychologists have discovered, are bigots. They turn their abnormally aroused state against mankind, particularly strangers. Any angry person, even one who can usually be described as reasonable, is likely to make bigoted statements while in an irate mood. Yale University made an interesting study of a group of young men who were anticipating an exciting evening's entertainment. The group was divided in two: one half was asked to express its attitude toward the Japanese and the other half its attitude toward Mexicans. Both groups were benignly inclined. Then the men were informed that the entertainment was canceled because some dull project was more pressing. The questionnaires then were switched, the first half were asked about Mexicans and the others about Japanese. This time animosity toward both races was recorded.

Angry adults are also negative. When asked about their opinions, they offer doubts, when asked about friends, they describe enemies and when asked about experiences tell of disappointments. Karen Horney, an outstanding psychoanalyst, observed of angry people that they tend "to demand power and prestige and personal infallibility as a major mode of coping with a hostile world." She noted exaggerated independence, ruthlessness and cynicism in the habitually angry, and a tendency to distrust and exploit others. If sexual prowess is important to them, angry men and women fill their lives with cold, mutilating conquests.

Sometimes entire nations will prefer a stern code in the raising of children, with the consequence that the whole population is suffused with anger. Anthropologist Margaret Mead found a tribe of head-hunters, the Iatmul, whose technique of caring for babies was to place them on a high distant shelf and leave them until they screamed with hunger. Small Iatmul children accordingly learned that anger is the only device to obtain comfort, and they possessed excruciatingly bad tempers.

Some hold that the reason Germans have been so superb in battle since the days of Caesar is the high level of anger in that race. Centuries of Christianity failed to eradicate the quality instilled by stiff discipline of children. As psychologist William McDougall pointed out, even the character of German religious thinkers reflects the national mood—Martin Luther was a wrathful and bellicose man.

Psychologist Alex Shand, in ticking off the types of mothers who produce the most angry children—cold, demanding ones, syrupy, coddling ones, self-righteous martyred ones—commented, "Large-minded tolerance, mixed with humor, reasonable perspective of small misdeeds, no nagging afterwards, these result in children who are less frequently angry."

But heredity, the dark horse in human personality whose influence isn't understood, may influence the anger in humans. Investigators have found that even brothers and sisters in the same family will have widely varying automatic responses, such as skin resistance, salivation, pulse and respiration, while identical twins will have almost the same responses. These differences in the neuroglandular system may be the factor that really determines how much anger will be innate, regardless of the good sense and good nature of the parents. On the other hand, every child (saving only identical twins) is raised in a different environment within the family. Middle children commonly are the angriest in the batch.

Around the turn of the century, when anger began to attract special attention in the emerging science of psychology, it was assumed that no one becomes angry unless his prevailing mood is discontent, self-dislike and irritation. Such a condition is typified by the man whose work at the office is going badly, whose drive home is through congested traffic and whose wife greets him indifferently. He blows up when he then is unable to find his newspaper.

But it soon became evident that anger emerges abruptly as well. Many people find themselves in an instantaneous fury, in the middle of a casual and pleasant afternoon. Such sudden rage is rarer than accumulative anger and has some peculiarities of its own. Mostly, it is caused by a circumstance linked with an unresolved childhood misery. The circumstance, like a conditioned reflex, *always* induces anger. A woman who was snubbed as a child always becomes angry when she encounters haughtiness; a man dominated by his mother and sisters cannot abide an authoritative female; another man who had reason not to trust his first friends will always react hotly to any disloyalty he imagines in his grown ones.

The most common display of anger is pugnacity. The

Roman philosopher Seneca composed the earliest known treatise on anger, describing its "glaring eye, wrinkled brow, violent motion, the hands restless and perpetually in action, wringing and menacing, the speech false and broken . . ." Henry Siddons in 1807 advised other actors to portray anger with an "inflamed and rolling eye, a heavy and impetuous step, increased speed of all body movements." Small children bite, as Charles Darwin noted, like "young crocodiles, who snap their little jaws as soon as they emerge from the egg." The baring of teeth typical of anger was believed by Darwin to be the lingering trace of primitive man's inclination to tear his enemies with his teeth; modern man's scowl is a residue, he added, of the fighting caveman's increased need for protection of his eyes.

According to University of Maine professor, Roy F. Richardson, in his *Psychology and Pedagogy of Anger*, the next most frequently employed display of anger is contrariness. About one fifth of the time, people in a temper will become overly polite and considerate with the person who has annoyed them. For this reason, excessive deference rightfully is suspicious.

The last, and least used, method of expressing anger is by indifference. People who react to an insult with a negligent shrug are no less angry than those who punch the offender in the nose. They may be demonstrating a paucity of resourcefulness. Incapable of shouting, possibly because they are afraid of their terrible anger, they can't think of any other means of retorting than to draw a veil over their faces. They appear unruffled, but they become monumental brooders.

The schemes of the angry are full of sadism. They plot without fatigue, while they drink coffee, prepare for bed, do the ironing, itemize a report. Their imaginations are lurid with withering monologues they picture themselves delivering to a cringing opponent, with the letter they will write that will *reveal all*, with deeds of revenge that in calmer moments are correctly judged to be demented. They can't pull their concentration to a happier subject; until the anger runs down, they are helpless.

During this period, angry people are treacherous to deal with. They may smile and joke, but their wit flays skin and nerves, their friendly claps on the back will break a rib and their generalizations will "inadvertently" insult the race, size, occupation or home town of the enemy. Meanwhile, their blood pressure is taking a beating that can shorten their lives. Anger has the effect in the body of increasing respiration and blood pressure and releasing adrenalin, which generates extra strength and the wealth of unhinged ideas. Blood vessels have a tendency to swell, especially the veins. Breathing becomes irregular and speech may be afflicted with stammering.

Suppressed anger, since it lasts longer than unleashed violence, does more damage internally. A report in the *Archives of General Psychiatry* noted that people who express their anger vocally don't suffer as great an increase in blood pressure and heart rate as those who swallow anger. Skin disorders are suspected to be the result of suppressed anger as well, and so are headaches and such other hypertension byproducts as ulcers, restlessness, fatigue and clumsiness.

Bottled anger is a hot, sour concoction that punishes every organ in the body. It is at its most disastrous state when the anger is turned against the self, which occurs frequently in cases where the mother has disciplined her child by the technique of appearing hurt or ill whenever the child misbehaved. In such cases, the child is made to feel guilty whenever he has offended and is shamefully angry at himself. When he grows to adulthood, he blames himself for every mishap or disappointment he encounters.

Many authorities share Karl Menninger's conviction that the gloom of depression is actually anger, directed inward because of an unreasonable compulsion not to show it outwardly. This theory is reflected in a treatment of attempted suicides pioneered by New York's Bellevue Hospital. Assuming that they are dealing with angry people who haven't been able to rid themselves in the normal way of their animosity, the staff handled them with coarse hostility. The startled patients reacted by lashing back with open tempers—and often, as a result, began to recover.

The rich anger that every man contains can't ever be pruned out; the dilemma lies in the proper handling of it. Some men convert their anger into achievement: Sigmund Freud was a cold, bitter and quarrelsome man but he opened the door to a universe. Sergeant York turned his bad temper into courage. John Calvin, his body ravaged by his anger, founded a religion to serve the angriest God in Christendom. Abraham Lincoln morosely turned his anger on himself and showed genius in his mildness.

"There is actually no productive activity into which some aggression does not enter in one way or another," commented psychoanalyst Melanie Klein. Work and play are both counted by psychiatry as useful outlets for anger, particularly such activities as golf, wood-chopping or scrubbing where hard blows are required.

But anger keeps spilling out. People in the process of liking themselves better have their maturing stopped cold when they commit a rash and spiteful deed. Self-respect becomes an impossibility for some time after a grown man finds himself a foot-stamping child again. When people are very angry, and realize that they wish to kill, they are terrorized by a fear of insanity so vivid that they feel dizzy.

The only answer to anger, the psychologists agree, is to lessen vulnerability. Once the personality is soundly matured and past the shoals of phoniness and suspicion, the individual isn't easily aroused by negligence or tactlessness in others. Mature people can tolerate their own failures realistically, without blaming others or punishing themselves sadistically, while the ineffectual at living are always at the mercy of mishaps.

Maturing is a long, tedious process, full of temporary reversals. In the interim, many have devised tactics to tame their anger. One method of recovering from a swell of anger is to try to gain a new concept of the situation, some additional information (facts were misunderstood, the opponent was quoted out of context). The other, less admirable technique which works just as well is to regain a sense of competence, which for the immature is derived from superiority.

Superiority is recovered in several ways. One is to clout the adversary senseless, a basic approach with a high social price. Civilization provides substitutes for mayhem: some regain their composure by doing their enemies a favor, thus reducing the dignity and value of the opponent; others feel better by spreading malicious gossip, or hinting at a scandal, or keeping ostentatiously silent while others are praising; still others apply the wrong end of a telescope to those who anger them, diminishing them with such belittlements as "he isn't very bright," "she doesn't understand this sort of thing," "he was acting out of jealousy," or "she is so unpopular, poor thing."

Anger is energy and must go somewhere. Relief can be obtained by going into an empty room and swearing fulsomely. Screaming is effective. A few people hum or sing tense little tunes. Others slam doors, distractedly tear a handkerchief, deliberately stumble against furniture, the breakable kind. Parents spank their children, which promptly relieves their anger but substitutes shame. Crying, which children universally use to release their intense anger, is also helpful to adults.

"Some persons have greater mental versatility than others in finding successful expressions of anger," remarked Maine's Professor Richardson. "Consequently they have a greater proportion of pleasantness."

An aim of many psychologists is to take the worry out of anger. "It is a normal emotional manifestation," Florence Goodenough observed. "It need cause anxiety only when it becomes excessive either in frequency or intensity, or when the attitudes aroused during anger show an undue tendency to persist in the form of grudges and feelings of persecution."

Anger can even be enjoyable. A man inflamed over injustice is delighted with himself; nothing is more beneficial to self-approbation than a good hearty rage over a clearly unfair act. "The anger of society," as William McDougall puts it, takes the form of ethics and law, a united righteous anger against wrong. Throughout the blooded world, anger defends the hearth; every species fights for its territory—springtime's songbirds, goats, elephants, moose, stickleback fish, wolves, rats and men.

"A large part of education is to teach men to be angry aright," declared the early U.S. psychologist G. Stanley Hall. "Man has powers of resentment which should be hitched onto and allowed to do good and profitable work."

Immanuel Kant mused two hundred years ago: "Man wishes concord, but nature knows better what is good for the species."

CHAPTER SIX

Ambition Is Mostly Neurotic

Ambition, the most admired of North America's neuroses, is mainly the direction that anger takes in the spirit of revenge for unappreciative parents, or social groups that excluded, or a real or imagined handicap. Ambition is rarely found in its healthy form: a zestful improvement of ability undertaken for the sake of the growth. Mostly, ambition is the compulsiveness that marks the immature.

The elements that combine to account for a monstrous ambition—the type known as a monkey on the back—usually include a certain sort of childhood. Psychologists find that highly ambitious adults generally suffered partial emotional deprivation as children. They received enough affection to give them a modest level of confidence, but so much scorn and rejection as well that they were unable to consolidate themselves.

The purposefulness conferred by misery during the early years has so impressed many parents that they fret because their children are being devotedly raised. Since the children can never experience brutality, abject poverty or ostracizing, it seems likely that they will be unremarkable adults, spine-lessly amiable and leisure-loving. Recent investigations, how-ever, demonstrate conclusively that the better the home environment, the brighter and more adventuresome the child. If they have the luck to receive affection and independence without strings, their ambition will flow happily from enthu-siasm and curiosity.

On mature ambition, Abraham Maslow, chairman of the psychology department at Brandeis University, has com-mented, "Capacities clamor to be used, and cease their clamor only when they are well used. Not only is it fun to use our capacities, but it is also necessary for growth. The unused skill or capacity or organ can become a disease center or else atrophy or disappear, thus diminishing the person."

The degree of ambition proclaims the man. Minimum ambition is concerned with sustenance alone, a low gear which is not restricted to the poor. Ambition directed at power, prestige and possessions, the most common kind, is based on anger and reinforced with hate. Psychoanalyst Karen Horney speaks of it as "moving against people." Ambition which involves self-realization is the highest form of the species and reflects a superior development of the personality.

Brooklyn College's department of psychology noted in 1948 that those whose ambition is mature show such qualities as "loyalty, friendliness and civic consciousness and become better parents, mates, teachers, etc." These people, the re-port continued, "love mankind the most and tend to be more individual and nonconforming."

Far from being blobs of contentment, adults who attain emotional maturity seem to be a yeasty lot, passionate about integrity and possessed of courage and judgment. Stanford University's vast *Studies of Genius*, published in the late twenties, observed, "Youths who achieve eminence are char-acterized not only by high intellectual traits but also by per-sistence of motion and effort, confidence in their abilities and great strength and force of character."

"All children love to learn," a seventy-year-old Virginian

schoolteacher remarked when she retired. "You can hardly keep them from learning."

Every normal baby possesses a great deal of curiosity; if it isn't damaged, he has enough to last a lifetime. Curiosity is all but killed in a child who receives his mother's hate and it is crippled in children who are overprotected and restrained from exploring their environment. The life style with which adults later approach new information and new situations is laid down in the freedom and safety provided for inquisitive babies.

The early American psychologist William McDougall speculated fifty years ago that the natural force of curiosity with which everyone is born operates something like a muscle—if it is flexed frequently, it becomes stronger and more useful, but if it is neglected, it shrinks.

Children who demonstrate a lively interest in learning generally seem to belong to homes where they were granted considerable liberty to touch and explore, while being shielded from dire consequences. The celebrated pediatrician Dr. Benjamin Spock suggests that about 75 per cent of the things a small child can reach in his home should be objects that are safe and permitted him; too many no's will lame a young, inquiring mind.

Overindulgence is almost as drastic a mistake with children as other, more open forms of cruelty. A child's ability to live in a natural world is reduced if he has no early practice at working out problems, enduring mild frustration and surmounting adversity. Little children need to teeth on small challenges in order to grow moral fiber. Success, or the discovery that failure is endurable, eventually makes them dauntless.

Laboratory animals have demonstrated this aspect of drive in a thousand experiments, possibly—since the North American is so incentive-conscious—tens of thousands of experiments. Slightly hungry or otherwise slightly deprived animals work vigorously; but, like humans, they quit altogether when the deprivation gets beyond their point of tolerance.

People with the highest level of tolerance are those with the maturity to value themselves realistically. A child can develop his sense of capableness in the judicious balance between protection and encouragement that his parents strike. A child who is pushed too hard and too soon becomes frantic. A McGill University survey in Montreal discovered that tough, aggressive fathers who bulled their way from shirtsleeves to wealth invariably had emotionally disturbed sons. "Fathers go for the jugular," commented the psychiatrist in charge of the study. Yale College's assistant dean, Richard C. Carroll, stated, "Somehow, in striving for brighter students—and getting them—we have increased the incidence of emotional instability."

One significant achievement test a few years ago found that many successful young people were children of mothers who expected them to be self-reliant at an early age—to make their own friends, to find their own way around their part of town, to do well in competitive sports. David C. McClelland, professor of psychology at Wesleyan University, pointed out that this training for self-reliance did not include what he termed "caretaking" items, such as putting oneself to bed, cutting one's own food, earning one's own spending money—"a fact which suggests that what was involved here was not rejection by the mother but rather a positive interest in the child's independence, growth and development."

(The redoubtable Kennedys were raised on the slogan: "When the going gets tough, the tough get going.")

Another achievement test demonstrated that outstandingly able children had in common a measure of independence before they were eight years old and the practice in their homes of giving rewards for accomplishment.

Environment exerts such an influence on the intelligence of children that some six-year-olds have gained fifty points on I.Q. tests by the time they reach the age of twelve and other six-year-olds have lost as much. A Fels Research Institute project at Antioch College in 1963 discovered that children with an increase in their I.Q.'s are more emotionally inde-

pendent of their parents, and come from democratic homes
that place a high value on education. Those children whose
I.Q.'s decrease as they grow older come from autocratic
homes, with domineering mothers and an emphasis in their
families on social functions and popularity.

Another primary factor is a measure of education provided
in the home before the child is of school age. Mothers who
read with their toddlers and fathers who instruct them while
toting them to museums, office buildings, factories, farms or
forests have a far-reaching effect on the child's intellectual
development. In 1910 a German chemist, Wilhelm Ostwald,
composed a list of the ten most important characteristics of
people who had shown surpassing talent in science. Early
training headed the list. A mammoth study of a thousand
men of science, conducted by J. McKeen Cattell, revealed
that the most distinguished of the scientists all had received
earlier education than the less distinguished ones.

Productive nations the world over have a general tendency
to educate their children early. After an absence of twenty-
five years, Margaret Mead revisited the South Seas tribes she
had studied as a young anthropologist and found that only
one of them, the Manus, had made the jump into the twentieth century. A United States Army base was near by and
the Manus had become hustlers, operating machinery, running a democratic government and setting themselves up as
bankers and businessmen for other tribes still too stunned to
participate in the boom. Miss Mead judged that the Manus
had adjusted quickly for one reason: the early independence
training of their young. The Manus live in houses built on
stilts over the water and tiny Manus children learn to swim
as soon as they can crawl and to handle canoes while still
toddlers.

There is some corroboration as well in a study of the myths
of various cultures. People who encourage their children at
an early age to master their environment seem to have myths
that are rich in achievement; people with no interest in the

early skills of their offspring have fearful myths, full of fantasy and magic but devoid of exploits.

Anthropologist Ashley Montagu states it firmly: "Where human beings tend to receive little or no assistance from their environment in the development of their potentialities, there will be little or no development of them. Where individuals tend to receive a mediocre or moderate kind of assistance from their environment, their potentialities will tend to be correspondingly developed. Where human beings receive a high degree of assistance from their environment, their potentialities will tend to be most highly realized."

All of this is in flat contradiction of the old concept that success is bred only out of hardship and pain. The recent emphasis on sympathy and respect in modern nurseries is also reflected in a fresh approach industry is taking with employees. The University of Iowa performed a classic experiment some years ago, assigning several groups of five boys to the task of making masks. Sometimes the groups were supervised by critical, angry, bossy leaders and sometimes by relaxed, helpful and friendly ones. It was expected by some that the casual leader would induce a spirit of sloth, while the perfectionist would step up production and efficiency, but it worked out exactly the opposite—discipline and output dropped under the tyrants and improved under the pleasant leaders.

Since then, there have been other controlled experiments with employees in such operations as a railway, a tractor factory and an insurance company. In every case, the teams with the best production and the sunniest workers were led by affable, considerate and co-operative men and women.

A benign environment, in fact, not only enables adults to work better but they can think more clearly. Untroubled by fear or irritation, their brains are able to function at their best. In the case of children, warmth and encouragement actually increases their intelligence. It has been observed that children raised in intellectually stunted circumstances, such as overcrowded institutions or with parents of very low intelligence, appear to be slow-witted. When they have been moved to a more stimulating environment, I.Q. increases of as much as thirty points can be obtained.

Parents who are university graduates and have maintained their intellectual vitality generally have brighter and more enterprising children than parents who don't read much and rarely discuss ideas. This proves to some that intelligence is inherited, and to others that intelligence is an elastic facility and responds to being stretched.

Scientists form only 3 per cent of the population, but J. McKeen Cattell found that half the scientists in the United States were descended from scientist fathers. Similarly, the respect that Jewish people have for learning is reflected in the fact that between 80 and 85 per cent of Jewish people in North America work in upper-level occupations, in which only 30 to 40 per cent of Gentiles are employed. It is also worthy of note that most of the prominent women in human history have lived during the past century, which was the first to respect and stimulate the minds of all female citizens.

"The old idea that genius will out despite any handicaps or restrictions is no longer tenable," writes University of Southern California's Norma V. Scheidemann in *Psychology of Exceptional Children.* "All indications are to the contrary. Environment is the great factor in releasing or hemming in innate ability."

David C. McClelland of Wesleyan University in 1951 described a survey of nursery school children. Those with the highest I.Q.'s, the most originality, playfulness and fancifulness came from what psychologists call "acceptant homes"; the most quarrelsome children came from rejectant homes and the most despondent ones from indifferent parents.

In *Personality,* Dr. McClelland reported on a famous study of identical twins, Johnny and Jimmy. One twin developed normally and the other was provided with early training in complicated skills. The twin with the ordinary upbringing caught up to his brother in some skills, such as skating, but the two had disparate attitudes when they grew up. The accelerated brother was vastly more confident in new situations, more receptive to change, more intrigued with new information.

The tone of the environment profoundly shapes the career choice of a young person. If there has been too much pressure on him to succeed, he may react with retaliatory idleness or else select a frivolous occupation. On the other hand, he may choose an occupation well ahead of his father's status and drive himself heartlessly to succeed at it. Dissension in the home sometimes induces a child to withdraw into daydreams, leading to a career as a writer, actor or artist. Of such people, Dr. Carl G. Jung once explained that their intensity toward the creative work they perform can result in the work outgrowing them. The work then becomes fully realized, profound and magnificent, while the creator remains childish, petulant and afraid. "The lives of artists," mused Dr. Jung, "are as a rule so highly unsatisfactory—not to say tragic—because of their inferiority on the human and personal side."

On the other hand, a good family life is apt to produce humanitarians, who hope to make a contribution through medicine, law, education, politics or social work. If they are gifted in music, drama, art or poetry, they are able to mature in step with their talent.

Except for those who show some early flair in a defined direction, all children go through a period in their early adolescence when only exciting jobs appeal. A group of high school teachers was surveyed a few years ago. All of them confessed ruefully that they had pined to be professional athletes, doctors, musicians, movie stars, railway engineers; teaching had been a secondary job choice.

A few fortunate children are so clearly endowed with a special skill that their lifetime work isn't in any doubt. Michelangelo was the despair of his father because he drew in the margins of his schoolbooks; like Rembrandt, Murillo, Raphael and Leonardo da Vinci, he was painting impressively before he reached puberty. Tennyson, Southey, Goethe and Emerson wrote acceptable poetry before they were ten. Mozart, the classic example of early promise, clearly was a genius when he was only three years old.

Some brilliant men, however, get off to a slow start. Winston Churchill was a poor student; one of Oliver Goldsmith's teachers claimed he was one of the dullest boys she had ever taught; Napoleon stood forty-second in his class; the philosopher Georg Hegel at university was judged "especially deficient in philosophy" and Woodrow Wilson didn't do well at Princeton.

Contemplating the late-bloomers, psychiatrists speculate that they were troubled as children but managed to achieve a later adjustment that released at least a part of their skill.

The golden period of a man's effectiveness is during his thirties. During this heightened decade, when experience has had time to inform judgment and energy is still youthful, most men do the best work of their lives. Harvey C. Lehman spent twenty years studying gifted men throughout history and found that their thirties were the most fruitful years. Writers, scientists, mathematicians, astronomers, artists, actors, philosophers, explorers, inventors, singers, composers, artists, psychologists, doctors, educators and geologists—all achieved what turned out to be their most important accomplishment while in their thirties.

Orators, architects, best-seller authors tended to be a little older, college presidents older still. Actresses, chemists and most athletes are younger when in their prime; poets have two good periods, in their twenties and again in their forties. Politicians, ambassadors and judges are at their peak between fifty-five and sixty; generals, bishops and heads of government between sixty and sixty-five. Popes make their mark in their eighties.

Lehman found that income isn't related to achievement, at least not at the time the major work was produced. In the main, men draw their best incomes thirty years after they have enjoyed their most remarkable period—in their late sixties. The delay is testimonial to civilization's chronic suspicion of the exploits of young men and women.

Civilization also enjoys feeling superior to superior people, and therefore delights in the maladjustment of some prominent people. The relentless inhumanity of most ambition renders the famous vulnerable to jeers. A person devoured by a need to succeed is willing to sacrifice health, leisure and family—but unwittingly throws in his wholeness and happiness as well. He makes a fine spectacle of his accomplishment and a shambles of his personality. The arts of tact, decency, sympathy and love require time to develop, reflection to polish, the courage of truthfulness to complete. Neurotics whose heads hold only ambition cannot be bothered.

Carl Jung proposed a budget theory about energy, that each man is born with a certain capital which he can invest as he chooses. Some put it all in one venture—fame—and therefore have nothing left over to give to the real prizes; self-respect, honor and friends. Overachievers with underdeveloped personalities account for most of the desolation in stately homes.

Psychoanalyst Alfred Adler's concept of human endeavor, that it flows from infantile rage at the primary discovery of helplessness and everlastingly aims at compensating the person for his first disadvantage, is true for many people. Napoleon was a short man (so was Adler) and underdogs are particularly dangerous foes, but few accidents of physiology give as much impetus to bitter ambition as does an unpleasant childhood. One selection of four hundred people, collected by Mildred G. and Victor Goertzel and published under the title *So They Had Problems Too*, found that most of them had a fiercely competitive mother and all felt inadequate and rejected.

The United States pioneer psychologist G. Stanley Hall once wrote: "Most of the greatest efforts I ever made in life were to escape inferiority and mediocrity."

Demosthenes, the orator who overcame a stammer, is a favorite Adler example. So is Annette Kellerman, physically frail as a child but an English Channel swimmer; the lame runner Nurmi; the weakling boy Eugene Sandow who was the world's strongest man. A few years ago Broadway's Julie Harris observed that if her chest had been bigger, she would not have needed to be so good an actress.

Few people ever work at the utmost of their ability. Harvard's William James once commented that a spur is needed in order to produce flat-out effort. Anger, which releases a torrent of energy into the human bloodstream, is certainly a formidable stimulus. The rage of a man scalded by his parents' disdain or desertion, or by a public humiliation, can carry him into a brilliant career. "Derogatory opinion," wrote Wayland F. Vaughan in *The Lure of Superiority*, "is a fertile seed for ambition."

Children who have failed to be loved may tear into a job at a velocity a notch or two above their natural speed. They may wind up in their middle age in a panic at their own acceleration and the falseness that maintains it. They have been hoping that power will give them protection against loneliness, which it never can do. Hollow, isolated successful people tend to cling together in a taut elite, maintaining their prestige only by keeping a good collection of necks under their heels.

"Domination springs from impotence," psychoanalyst Erich Fromm claims. The man infatuated with money and power acts "under the illusion that his actions benefit his self-interest, though he actually serves everything else *but* the interests of his real self." His power corrupts him ultimately, because he can compel phony loyalty and companionship without bothering to qualify himself in the normal way, by personal worth.

There is no possibility of attaining happiness by the sheer accumulation of money and fame, the pursuit of which is replete with doubt, envy and depression. The flares of triumph, occurring intermittently, never take off the curse of ambition. Many of the world's most dazzling men and women are hooked on the thrill of triumph; they are work addicts, socially acceptable but not more sound than drug or alcohol addicts. The obsessively ambitious can be grouped with the other obsessions which border on mental illness.

Three hundred years ago Benedict Spinoza declared, "If the greedy person thinks only of money and possessions, and the ambitious one only of fame, one does not think of them as being insane . . . but, factually, greediness, ambition and so forth are forms of insanity." Nietzsche called ambition "the evil breath" and commented bitterly, "See how they climb, these swift apes! They climb over one another, and thus drag themselves in the mud and depths." Judge Learned Hand, one of the greatest of the United States judiciary, called ambition "Satan's apple."

A different interpretation of Adler's compensation theory is that ambition actually is a form of love-seeking. The Scottish psychiatrist Ian D. Suttie is a leading exponent of this and asserts, "The quest for admiration is one of the earliest adopted of all the false starts or blind alleys of social development."

It can begin with children who are able to attract their parents' attention only when they excel, and therefore winning becomes their only goal. Montreal psychiatrist Karl Stern notes the prevalence of stomach trouble in many successful people, those hard-driving victims of perfection. "Deep down," he writes, "such people have a great need to receive; they are people whose hard spartan shell covers a yearning to be mothered." Mothering equates with feeding, which accounts for the prevalence of peptic ulcers.

The longing to be love-worthy, combined frequently with some degree of Adlerian power drive, delivers up a host of despondent giants. Asked how he was able to discover his mechanical system of the universe, Isaac Newton answered, "By thinking about it day and night." Abraham Lincoln's advice to young lawyers was "Work, work, work . . . your own resolution to succeed is more important than any other one thing." And Charles Darwin explained, "It's doggedness that does it."

No list of the world's great men would be complete without these names, but all were estranged from the world.

Lincoln suffered from melancholy so severely that many have judged him on the borderline of sanity; Newton sulked like a teen-ager because he wasn't given state office and Darwin was so afraid of his father's disapproval that he put off publishing his world-changing theory of evolution for twenty-six years after he had formulated it.

"We wholly overlook the essential fact that the achievements which society rewards are won at the cost of the diminution of personality," Carl Jung maintained. The dehumanizing of the ambitious occurs when they are so meager of development that they can nourish only one asset, abandoning family, friendships, recreation and meditation. They add a mite of exploit somewhere but destroy themselves.

The consequence of those who put ambition in the perspective of their lifetime goal of worth is a rich existence. Without having to stoop to the theatrics of martyr dedication, the wholesomely ambitious accomplish their best, keep their friends, adore their families. They emerge gloriously in the round, awesome in their central integrity. In his Terry lectures at Yale in 1955, Gordon W. Allport discussed what he calls propriate striving, the drive of the mature man. "Propriate striving distinguishes itself from other forms of motivation in that, however beset by conflicts, it makes for the unification of the personality," he said.

Propriate striving involves risk-taking, he explained, since people with sound personalities haven't much concern for protecting their egos and taking the safe route. It is not rewarded, as the neurotics expect, with fulfillment, or repose, or reduced tension. Mature people don't require such lollipops, being essentially fulfilled, at ease and exhilarated. The measure of intellectual maturity, as philosopher C. W. Churchman has commented in a score of famous-quotation collections, is our ability to feel less and less satisfied with our answers to better and better problems.

Failure to develop inner resources as the external facilities improve leads to horror, which the vulgar inventory of notoriety, good address, attractive family and homage cannot relieve. Unfortunately, all these are equated with happiness; an assumption which is the leading fallacy of this age.

Carl Jung called maturity "inner spaciousness." "Without the inner breath," he wrote, "we are never related to the size of our object. It is therefore right to say that a man grows with the size of his task. But he must have within him the ability to grow, otherwise the most difficult task will be of no use to him; at the most he will break himself upon it."

The man whose growth contains his ambition is a marvel, but the man whose ambition grows without him is ill, poor devil.

CHAPTER SEVEN

Happiness Exists

Happiness is the rarest, most prized and most misunderstood state of man. Happiness in North America is widely believed to be a glossy four-color reproduction of hearty, handsome parents beaming in a landscaped garden where starched children play dreamily with new toys. Throw in such additional bonbons as a blue sky, an electric dishwasher, relief from constipation and a passionate love affair and it might add up to five minutes of happiness.

Lasting happiness is what's inside the human skin. It's related to how much maturity a man has been able to assemble, some of it derived from being desperately unhappy. It's a consequence of at least a moderate amount of education or training, because happiness requires a decently stocked mind. It's bound up with the ability to work, to find a lot to do, to be readily interested.

It also is part of an unembarrassed appreciation of leisure and of solitude. A sense of religion is usually present in happy people, and so is a discriminating eye for folly, which often disguises itself as nobility. Most of all, happiness is attached to those dispositions which are prone to give welcome, a trait reflected in snug family life, enduring friendships and the regard of strangers.

Happy people can be any age, past twenty. Children are rarely happy: they have flights of joy but their helplessness in an adult world that disappoints and restricts—"dependent as a slave" as William Lyon Phelps put it—keeps them close to despondency. Until their personalities stablilize, a process generally completed after the age of thirty-five, they are likely to be wretched with self-doubts, loss of religious faith and dismay at their inner muddle.

When a thousand elderly people were questioned in a research project, they claimed that their happiest years had been between the ages of twenty-five and forty-five, news that astonished the harried group presently occupying those years. Young adults may describe themselves as "happy"; it's a serviceable word to protect privacy. But many of them are frantic at the acceleration of time they are beginning to feel. They can sense the years wheeling by without any substantial accomplishment, or one that gives them satisfaction. They seem to be plucked by a million selfish fingers until their flesh aches. Grieving over their mistakes and wrong choices, they don paper hats for laughs, give anxious parties, drink too much, talk too much and say too little. They see old age as a catastrophe, a final bad joke on the false dream of being happy.

Yet all over the world, men and women, most of them in their thirties, are turning a corner that they didn't see, and stand transfixed by the miracle of finding themselves happy. Nothing has changed in the room, in the family; nothing anywhere is different—but everything seems so. Happiness is unmistakable. One woman compared it with the unequivocal quality of a genuine labor pain. "When you're carrying your first baby," she explained, "you keep wondering what a labor pain is like. Every time you have a cramp or twinge you wonder if this is it. Then eventually you have a whopper of a labor pain. There is no question in your mind about it, you *know* that this positively is the real thing. Well, becoming happy is just the same. You think you are from time to time in your life, but when it really arrives you recognize it immediately."

The personality has put together enough experience to make sane judgments, enough vitality to love, a great deal of self-appraisal, a few fragments of clarity and courage. There is a soundless click, and a steady state of happiness is produced.

Nearly thirty years ago a radio series on a United States network dealt with human happiness. It drew an astonishing response, the most striking feature of which was that some people wrote that they were happy in the identical circumstances which were reducing other correspondents to depression and self-pity. Precisely the same deformity had one woman wailing inconsolably in one part of the country, while another woman a thousand miles away was bubbling with what seemed sincere praise for the kindness of people around her.

Psychologists have been slow to study happiness; most of them didn't believe it existed. Now they are putting together some studies of mature, happy adults with their old favorite, babies and young children. They find that some of the necessary qualifications for eventual happiness are built into babies. Infants with good-natured, fond mothers enjoy themselves and are readily intrigued and amused, faculties which are the foundation of a sensible and educated mind.

No one is born happy. The first discernible human emotions are negative ones—anger, fear and hatred at the inevitable discomforts of infancy. The infant first responds to warmth and food by being quiescent, though he may smile involuntarily as early as the fourth day. But by the third month, babies are really pleased to be cuddled and they smile at every human face.

The responsive smiles of babies, the first entrancing show of happiness, have been studied by many scientists, notably Dr. René A. Spitz, with Dr. K. M. Wolf. They could observe a universal human pattern: until the age of six months, babies of every race will smile at any friendly adult, almost without exception. Mankind shows its instinctive sociability in the fact that babies infrequently smile at toys or feeding bottles, but almost always smile at people.

The researchers discovered that babies will smile at a hideous grimace, so long as the teeth are bared, the forehead smooth and the head nodding occasionally. They also smile meltingly at Halloween masks and scarecrows that fulfill the same conditions, but they will never smile back at a face with one eye or both covered, never smile at a profile and soon stop smiling if the face doesn't move.

One baby girl being examined by psychologists smiled in response to a smile when she was only twenty-five days old. She promptly became a favorite. It was found that she was emotionally mature for her age; by the time she reached her first birthday she was a full four months ahead of her chronological age in development. Dr. Spitz explained that she had an "unusually pleasant and devoted mother."

Institutionalized, love-starved babies don't smile at a smiling face; they make up almost all the exceptions to the rule. Dr. Spitz concluded that they had been unable to reach even an elementary stage of social development but remain essentially newborns—narcissistic and capable only of quiescence as their highest pleasure. Lonely babies, raised by self-preoccupied mothers or by a string of mother-substitutes, may grow up permanently retarded in their emotional unfoldment. Since they haven't known even the fringe of happiness, they assume it must belong only to those with possessions or fame. A lifelong, hopeless pursuit of gain can result.

Even the most fortunate of babies is joyful only intermittently, and for superficial reasons. Adolescents are surpassingly unhappy a good deal of the time, even when their homes are friendly. Young married couples and people at the beginning of their careers are distracted by novelty and challenge and rarely give a thought to happiness. Then momentum gathers behind them, the various personalities they have been using at whim all seem monstrous and their middle years are approaching in a gathering dark horror.

According to psychoanalyst Erich Fromm, happiness is an achievement, brought about by inner productiveness. "It is not," he declares firmly, "a gift of the gods." People succeed at being happy in the same way they succeed at loving, by building a liking for themselves for true reasons. Hollow people, lacking any conviction of their worth and without self-respect, have nothing to give—a profoundly unhappy state. They must connive to secure love and admiration for themselves and they can't depend on keeping it. The self-flatterers, on the other hand, are practicing a deception they acknowledge in their depths; their enmity against the world is the dread that everyone is on to them.

Aristotle believed that the definition of happiness is self-sufficiency, a sentiment echoed with a mathematician's spareness by Benedict Spinoza, who wrote three hundred years ago: "Happiness consists in this: that man can preserve his own being."

One of the most often quoted comments on happiness was made by Timothy Dwight, in a speech when he was president of Yale University. "The happiest person," he declared, "is the person who thinks the most interesting thoughts." William Lyon Phelps was greatly impressed by this and was moved to develop it. "The principle of happiness is like the principle of virtue," he reflected. "It is not dependent on things, but on personality."

He added, "You will have days and nights of anguish, caused by ill health or worry or losses or the death of your friends, but you will not remain in the Slough of Despond, you will rise above the depression and disaster because you will have in your mind the invincible happiness that comes from thinking interesting thoughts."

One of the world's most respected psychologists, William McDougall, has a parallel comment: "The richer, the more highly developed, the more completely unified or integrated is the personality, the more capable it is of sustained happiness, in spite of intercurrent pains of all sorts."

One American writer announced that he had been a happy man every day of his adult life. Of course, he admitted, there had been days when he was jobless and hungry, days of grief over a bereavement, days of nausea and illness—but on each one of them he had been able to contact the deepest part of himself which was operating steadily, soundly and happily.

The relationship between happiness and maturity defeats the rationalization of many aging adults—that happiness is youth and naturally diminishes with time. Bertrand Russell, when ninety, claimed he grew happier every year. Joseph H. Choate, a nineteenth-century U.S. diplomat, insisted that the happiest time of life is between seventy and eighty. He told an audience crisply, "I advise you all to hurry and get there as soon as you can." On his ninety-fifth birthday, the Canadian educator Sir William Mulock said serenely, "I am still at work, with my hand to the plow and my face to the future. . . . The first of May is still an enchanted day to me." He saw six more first of Mays.

Philosophers have been making the same point for centuries. Plato thought of youth as a troubled time, and old age as the best "because at last a man is freed from the animal passion which has hitherto never ceased to disquiet him." But the regrets of an old man who lived to be eighty echo ruefully down the years. Plato went on, "Yet it should not be forgotten when this passion is extinguished the true kernel of life is gone, and nothing remains but the hollow shell; or, from another point of view, life becomes a comedy which, begun by real actors, is continued and brought to an end by automata dressed in their clothes."

Studies of the aged, an ever increasing proportion of North American population, show that their happiness seems to depend entirely on how busy they are. If they have some ability to work well, have kept family ties, friendships, hobbies and other interests, they are among the elite. One survey of a thousand people between the ages of sixty and one hundred discovered that most of them said they were happy between the ages of sixty and sixty-four when they still felt useful, but after that, particularly with men, a decline began.

Throughout their lives, most people think happiness is a gimmick. They search for it sometimes in drunkenness ("temporary suicide," Bertrand Russell calls it, "making life bearable by being less alive"). Sadistic people think happiness is domination, but they never get enough of it; masochists seek humiliation and overwork. Fearful people, greedy people, envious people think happiness is wealth or repute. The possessive covet human sacrifice, the near-impotent claw for sexual conquest—and all of it in quest of happiness.

Unhappy people rarely blame themselves for their condition. Their jobs are at fault, or their marriages, or the meanness of fate, the vileness of parents, the disgusting handiwork of aging. But the real cause of their wretchedness is the incoherency of their lives. Sterile and confused, they have no warmth to give work, play or love. They wait in apathy for a visit from the Fairy Godmother, and in the meantime try to distract their attention from the abyss of barrenness and boredom within them. The farthest notion from their minds is to improve their lot by tackling some self-reconstruction.

The world over, faces in a crowd are rarely joyant. Travelers, shoppers, idlers pass one another looking worried, or listless, or buttoned to the eyes in blankness. In social groups men and women tend to smile almost constantly and they laugh a good deal. It's a mirth that doesn't interrupt the progress of an ulcer. Without happiness, life tastes like bad meat.

Some people fall into a stretch of happiness during their lives by some fluke they can never duplicate again. It lights a glow that looks ever brighter in retrospect, a poignancy that makes men wistful. Many people have no protracted happiness at all. Sophocles wrote the bitter line, "Count no man happy who is not dead."

Nothing on earth renders happiness less approachable than trying to find it. Historian Will Durant described how he

looked for happiness in knowledge and found only disillusionment. He then sought happiness in travel and found weariness, in wealth and found discord and worry. He looked for
happiness in his writing and was only fatigued. One day he
saw a woman waiting in a tiny car with a sleeping child in
her arms. A man descended from a train and came over and
gently kissed the woman and then the baby, very softly so
as not to waken him. The family drove off together and left
Durant with a stunning realization of the real nature of happiness. He relaxed and made the discovery that "every normal
function of life holds some delight."

When Admiral Richard E. Byrd believed himself to be
dying in the ice of the Ross Barrier, he wrote some thoughts
on happiness. "I realized how wrong my sense of values had
been and how I failed to see that the simply, homely, unpretentious things of life are the most important . . . When
a man achieves a fair measure of harmony within himself
and his family circle, he achieves peace . . . At the end only
two things really matter to a man, regardless of who he is:
they are the affection and understanding of his family."

The rasping Frenchman La Rochefoucauld concluded,
"when we cannot find contentment in ourselves, it is useless
to seek it elsewhere."

"The typical unhappy man," said philosopher Bertrand
Russell, "is one who, having been deprived in his youth of
some normal satisfaction more than any other, has given to
his life a one-sided direction with a quite undue emphasis on
the achievement, as opposed to the activity connected with
it." Lord Russell, suicidally unhappy as a youth, gradually
cured himself of it by giving up his preoccupation with himself and turning his interest outward.

A permeating, permanent state of happiness is rare, but the
world abounds in welcome fragments. There is the calm happiness of an old woman baking pies, the bliss of a boy with
a good report card, the shaft of ecstasy that goes through a
winner. There are also what Dr. Fromm calls the lower
pleasures of satisfying a physical need—eating, sleeping, elim-

ination, sex, exercise. The higher pleasures are derived, he explains, from usefulness, self-possession and the growth of insight.

Abraham Maslow describes the higher pleasures as sensations of "functioning easily, perfectly, at the peak of one's powers—in over-drive, so to speak." In the state of happiness, all physical and mental faculties seem to exceed themselves.

A housewife who crossed over to a state of happiness in her thirty-sixth year, for no reason she could ever name, was startled by the intensity of her vision on several occasions. Lawns would become separate blades of grass, each one distinct and infinitely graceful, trees were full of separate leaves and tiny clear objects floated enchantingly on rain puddles. Tolstoi recorded the same phenomenon in *Anna Karenina* when the hero Levin steps into the street after his love has promised to marry him. He encounters a more vivid sky than he has ever seen, faces in the streets seem full of nobility and kindness, ordinary noises have a textured clarity. The Irish novelist Brian Moore, in *The Luck of Ginger Coffey*, describes Coffey's rapture at being found innocent of a sordid crime; it takes the form of an inspired oneness with a good world, a blending of himself and infinity.

Joy is such a feeling of lightness that a doctor in 1775 declared emphatically that happiness causes a decrease in body weight. The sense of heady lightness, however, is derived prosaically from improved circulation which supplies such rich blood to the muscles and brain that they become supple and full of buoyant vitality. This bountiful nourishment accounts for the slow aging of happy people. They have better color, glossier skins, more erect carriage than their contemporaries, who suffer the graying atrophy of depression and anxiety.

The lusty flow of blood typical of happiness is particularly stimulating to the brain, which perceives smells, sounds and sights that never had separate identity before. "Increased circulation brightens the eye," enthused Charles Darwin, "color rises, lively ideas pass rapidly through the mind, affections are warmed." He catalogued the benefits: lifted head, erect body, improved digestion, smooth brow, arched eyebrows, wide-open eyelids.

Dr. Elizabeth Bagshaw, a Canadian woman who continued her medical practice when she was past eighty, was interviewed when curling one day and declared, "People who are happy usually have a better degree of health than people who worry." A psychologist who questioned five hundred young men to determine their degree of happiness made the not unexpected discovery that happiness and health generally go together. Happy people are ill less often, recover more quickly, even have bones and tissue that heal better. The dark emotions, hate, anger, fear, depression and guilt, all are destructive to organs, lowering immunity to infections, causing interior pain and malfunctioning, impoverishing tissues.

Early philosophers who considered the enigma of happiness evolved a theory that pain is bad for man and pleasure is beneficial, *ergo* the sensible man should avoid all pain and partake of as much pleasure as he can find. Hedonism continues to appeal strongly to children of all ages. Epicurus, an abstemious Greek whose name has come to stand for indulgences he deplored, noted the singular misery of such pleasure-soaked creatures as drunks, misers, opportunists and rakes. He was the first to suggest that *some* pleasures are decidedly harmful to man, while some pain is indisputably healthful.

Theology and philosophy ever since have closed ranks with this proposition—happiness truly is derived from those dull chestnuts, virtue and wisdom. To these psychology adds one more, productiveness.

Wise, virtuous, productive men, finding themselves happy, have tried to fathom the mystery of it. They cannot agree. Charles Darwin declared for domestic affection and the study of nature; Oliver Wendell Holmes revered frequent contact with quick and well-stored minds. He also said, "To live is to function. That's all there is to living." Socrates and Thomas Jefferson believed that human happiness comes from the intellect. "What is without us has no connection with happiness," Benjamin Franklin declared. "Happiness springs immediately from the mind." Voltaire considered that work was happiness and Francis of Assissi thought it was sparsity of comfort.

Oddly, laughter has little or no relationship to the state of happiness. Laughter is judged by behavior specialists to be a not exclusively human method of relieving tension, which can accompany any acute emotion. While people laugh when they are comfortable with old friends, laugh at the expressions on the faces of children they adore, chuckle readily when they are feeling good, they also will titter when they are desperately afraid, show hatred when they roar at malicious jokes, make a valiant show of gaiety when they are despondent. Lincoln, who suffered agonies of depression, commented, "If I did not laugh, I should die." Voltaire, the happiest of all philosophers, said he laughed in order to avoid madness.

It was Freud's humorless notion that humor is a foil for repressed loathing. He cited as an example Will Rogers, who used to declare that he never met a man he didn't like, but spent his days composing daggers. Humor is so effective at siphoning off hatred that men without it are brutes. The playwright Eugène Ionescu wrote, "Where there is no humor, concentration camps arise, and where there is no laughter, we see anger and hate."

Stephen Leacock, Canada's most celebrated humorist, suggested that laughter originated as a primitive shout of triumph and has been civilized only superficially, so that society condones laughing at minor misfortunes only. Certainly the enjoyment of the clumsiness of clowns stems from an agreeable sense of superiority.

"The humor of healthy people produces a smile, rather than a laugh," noted Geoffrey Leytham in *World*. "It is philosophic and not based on hostility, aggression or superiority. Their jokes are like parables, they teach as well as amuse, and rarely hurt anybody. If they poke fun at others or themselves it is not due to sadism or masochism but as a way of keeping things in their true perspective."

Tears are as poor an indicator of sadness as laughter is of happiness. People weep when they grieve, but also when they fear, hate, are outrageously angry or full of joy. Penelope sighted her husband Ulysses after twenty years of faithful waiting and "from her eyelids quick tears did start." James Thurber wrote that perfection in comedy causes a "curious and instantaneous tendency of the eyes to fill."

Temple University's Professor Frederick H. Lund believed that tears are a distinctly pleasant outlet for accumulating energy. He found weeping particularly effective when the emotions are mixed and thwart one another in such a tangle that exasperated weeping is vastly satisfying—as in the case of mothers attending weddings or when lovers fight.

Calm, serene happiness rarely laughs or cries (Lord Chesterfield thought both bad form for a gentleman, in any case). It has too much stability to need the tools of the tense. It is embodied in the private conquest of self-dislike and the honesty of self-definition. Walter Lippmann in 1929 wrote A *Preface to Morals,* in which he outlined his concept that maturity, happiness, is the harmony within the individual.

"In the womb and for a few years of his childhood," he wrote, "happiness was the gratification of the person's naive desires. His family arranged the world to suit his wishes . . . As he grows up he can no longer hope that the world will be adjusted to his wishes, and he is compelled by a long and difficult process of learning and training to adjust his wishes to the world." He derives, from what seems like surrender, the jubilance Norman Mailer once described as "something in oneself coming up free of the muck."

A Frenchman once said that wise men are happy with trifles, but nothing pleases fools. All wise men, however, have been fools; they convert themselves by several methods.

Count your blessings—only numskulls are tormented by regrets and recriminations, advised Cicero. Pause to enjoy—Goethe, a craftsman at happiness, explained that happiness is not transitory joy, but a longevity of secret power. Sharpen your wits when you observe man and nature, because understanding the unique strength and beauty within all living things is the heart of happiness. Never fear to use yourself up. The great elixir of life, according to George Bernard Shaw, is to be thoroughly worn out before being discarded on the scrap heap—"a force of nature, instead of a feverish, selfish clod of ailments and grievances." Never delay; unhappiness is nurtured by the habit of putting off living until some fictional future day.

Dr. Fromm proclaimed, "Happiness is proof of partial or total success in the art of living." There are few successes. "The art of life is the most distinguished and rarest of all the arts," said Dr. Jung. But not impossible. Never, never impossible.

CHAPTER EIGHT

The Blues Are Demi-Death

Melancholia, whether it lasts an afternoon because the picnic is rained out, or through thirty years of bleakness, is the emotion which tilts a man toward death. It crushes vitality and turns the sun black; it happens to everyone.

It is the state of man when he has fallen below his own expectations. It can be brought about by a financial setback, a death or merely a silence that wounded. Some people can recover their tranquillity after an interval—a minute, a year— but others have the tone of death all their lives. Depression is the emotional equivalent of quitting. It damages the body severely and accelerates aging.

Some people, including many of the world's greatest figures, have an underlying quality of melancholy that makes them tender of their fellow man. Aristotle noted twenty-three hundred years ago that poets, philosophers, politicians and artists "appear to be all of a melancholic temperament." Jesus Christ was sad and Abraham Lincoln endured so much depression that he was nearly insane. It was known as "the

English malady" in the days when Charles Dickens groveled under the weight of it.

Depressions are the bass notes in a lifetime. The orchestration of living would be brassy without them, for they induce introspection and assessment. Teen-agers couldn't mature without the blues, which provide the insights vital to growth. Most of the aged are afflicted with them, but to no good purpose. They also accompany illness and all human excesses, even sunburn. Babies are particularly susceptible; psychotic states of depression have been observed in three-month-old infants.

Despite the fact that the clinical details of depression were outlined in 400 B.C. by the father of medicine, Hippocrates, only in recent years have the scientists been able to explain why some people are sadder than others.

A prevailing mood of depression is rarely the reflection of adult misfortunes, it seems, but the result of a certain kind of childhood. A conference on depression in 1959 at McGill University, Montreal, attended by psychiatrists from all over the world, found agreement that the classic pattern of a person suffering chronic depression is a happy infancy, during which he received good mothering, and then an abrupt transition at the age of one, when he was required to meet standards beyond his capabilities.

Mothers who impose stiff and unrealistic discipline on their toddlers are either frantically concerned with the good opinion of their neighbors or else are domineering perfectionists, who punish themselves with their abnormal rules and destroy the pride of their families. From the baby's point of view, he was born into a marvelous world which suddenly ends because— as he perceives from his mother's disapproval—he is no longer worthy. He strives to recover the blissful state he once enjoyed, by the method pointed out to him: perfect behavior. This is beyond his ability, naturally, so he feels he is a failure. Before he is two years old, he has the desolating conviction that he isn't lovable.

This psychic mutilation occurs most frequently in middle-class homes, among suburbanites who compete with one another by means of their children's accomplishments and courtesies. It is commonest still in the first-born of families in every class, since the first child is a living testing ground for all the crackpot child-raising theories that new parents can invent. The product is an adult who is excessively ingratiating, since he already has had more ill opinion than he can tolerate. The women become meticulous, highly organized tyrants, who demand model friends, husbands and children and therefore contaminate another generation with their hopelessness. The men are fastidious, punctual, conscientious, driving workers, respected but not much liked.

Almost two thousand years ago the scientist Aretaeus described the melancholy as guilt-ridden, religious and sacrificing. He has had corroboration through the years. Recently Robert O. Jones, professor of psychiatry at Dalhousie University in the Canadian Maritimes, informed some of his associates that the Scottish Calvinists in the area produced a bumper crop of depressions. Depressions are epidemic among the followers of harsh religions, the admirers of superhuman conduct, the misfortunate for whom second prize is no prize at all.

Gross overdevelopment of the conscience is so typical of melancholia that one English psychiatrist, Edward Glover, refers to it as "chronic hyperplasia [overgrowth] of the superego [conscience]." Mostly though, depression is known as "a complete or partial loss of self-esteem." It is the state of the unfortunate one-year-old who can't please his mother, but it can happen to babies even younger.

Newborn babies are acutely vulnerable to any slur on their importance. An infant discovers if he is valuable or not by measuring the loyalty and friendliness of the person who tends him. If she is indifferent, or restricts his freedom, or if the faces around him keep changing before he can get accustomed to their habits, he concludes he isn't worth much. He is profoundly discouraged, and droops physically and emotionally.

If a child can reach the age of three without falling into a pattern of moroseness, it seems likely that he will be reasonably free of neurotic depression for the rest of his life. Studies of small children in hospitals show some interesting types. Below the age of three, well-loved children suffer a violent reaction at being separated from home. They become withdrawn, seem to be in a dazed stupor, sleep poorly and lose weight. When their parents visit, they sometimes turn their heads away in misery. After the age of three, they are able to tolerate separation without such personality disintegration. Children who are not accustomed to affection, however, are relatively unmoved by hospitalization at any age.

The mother-baby relationship is almost certainly the thermostat that controls the level of melancholia in a lifetime. The pessimist philosopher Schopenhauer was the victim of a mother who hated him so much she once pushed him down a flight of stairs. He wrote sullenly, "The only honest wish man can have is that of absolute annihilation." Lord Byron's mother also treated him abominably and made him a gloomy man.

The entertainment business is particularly attractive to the melancholy. Comedians and clowns, especially, are usually depressed individuals who try to warm themselves on audience laughter. The theological scholar Paul Tillich tells the famous story of the doctor who was treating a patient for melancholy. "You need amusement," he told him. "Go and hear Grimaldi. He will make you laugh and that will be better for you than any drugs." The patient was horrified. "My God!" he cried, "but *I* am Grimaldi!"

Jack Benny, for instance, can't shake his loneliness; neither can such disparate humorists as Red Skelton and Shelley Berman. Mark Twain, Molière, Jonathan Swift, Danny Kaye—all are deeply sad men. They hope to gain the sense of worthiness they missed as babies, when it would have been easy to acquire, by being popular as adults, when their chances are decidedly poor.

Freud believed that the feeling of inferiority that lacerates the melancholy is essentially the fear of being unloved, of being incapable of inspiring pure love. Depression in adults is a complexity of many emotions: hatred and anger against the self, which never comes up to the dream; deep fear of disapproval, rejection, loneliness, the unknown; guilt over social failures, blurted cruelties, selfishness; infantile greed for more than is due; envy of everyone with an advantage, which for the melancholy means nearly everyone. The chronically depressed need only their own approval, some honorable proof of goodness, to emerge. But if they missed the knack of it back when they learned to walk, it is excruciatingly difficult to learn.

Few people, however, are unrelentingly depressed, at least until their very old age. The least depressed time of life is around the age of ten, but after this everyone experiences flickers of depression. The adolescent years, when the child's body dismayingly becomes a stranger, are particularly de-pression-prone. So too are all the years of massive rumblings and settling, such as early in a marriage or parenthood and during the change-of-life years. Partly because of the sense of strangeness it provokes, glandular change in the body always involves a depressive spell. Pregnant women experience it, sometimes acutely, and go through it again in the postnatal period.

The giving up of dreams is also a desolating milestone. When ideals and ambitions turn out to be absurdities, the soul is shocked. Goethe commented sympathetically on youth "that hurls itself madly against the windmills and evils of the world, and sadly sheds its Utopias and ideals with every year."

The middle years are fertile for depression because many maintain their confidence with such summer soldiers as attractiveness and potency. Women who existed for their children, thus badly mangling their young, must face empti-ness when the family grows. Men who were too busy establish-ing careers find that their wives and children are distant and unforgiving. Both sexes have a menopause, marked by bodies that are soft, thick and dry-skinned.

As old age approaches, the capacity to respond to pleasure decreases. Depression is easily triggered; any excitement or crisis sets it off. Eventually, in those old people who were unable to develop their emotional resources during their twenties and thirties, the attacks of gloom merge and become perpetual until death.

Not all depression shows itself in a mournful face. Teenagers, for instance, generally are sarcastic and cheerful-seeming. One doctor suggested that parents watch for such danger symptoms as intense excitement over trivialities, along with a negligent attitude toward important matters; overwhelming fatigue; obsessive fascination for newness. All these can indicate a high degree of concealed melancholia.

Adults sometimes hide their blues under a giddy display of gaiety. In the hope of entertaining themselves, they reel off rough jokes and protest noisily when the party breaks up. They exhaust themselves, a condition which increases their depression.

The majority of depressions are what doctors term endogenous, or arising from within the personality. They range from the grinding blackness of a psychotically depressed person who wants to kill himself to those free-floating wisps of discontent that render poetry more poignant. The difference between a depression that is a certifiable mental illness and one that is bittersweet, and rather comforting, is solely one of degree; the symptoms in either case are the same: loss of appetite, sleeplessness, inability to concentrate.

The symptoms also apply in the other category of depression, the exogenous ones that follow a sorrow. These trace a classic course—the initial numbness and disbelief, then heavy, hard grief, then gradually reviving interest in other matters and finally, six months to a year later, a not unpleasant nostalgia. The strong, wrenching emotion of a new grief is a form of energy that demands release. Psychologists find enduring wisdom in the ancient Hebraic injunction: "Do not

hasten to rid a friend of his grief." The work of grief, screaming, crying, distributing the dead one's possessions, are valuable restoratives. Mrs. Jacqueline Kennedy's singular control
during her most public widowhood was made possible in part,
by the hyperclarity and activity of her mental processes; the
plans and decisions of those first days after President John F.
Kennedy's assassination served his widow as a substitute for
hysteria.

Grief must out, in one form or another. Psychiatrist
Erich Lendemann of the Harvard School of Medicine once
commented, "The duration of a grief reaction seems to depend upon the success with which a person does the grief
work, namely emancipation from the bondage to the deceased, readjustment to the environment in which the
deceased is missing and the formation of new relationships.
One of the big obstacles to this work seems to be the fact
that many patients try to avoid the immense distress connected with the grief experience and to avoid the expression
of emotion necessary for it."

Sorrow inhibits the muscles, generating a feeling of lassi-
tude. The head droops and the face sags, heavy-lidded. The
voice becomes weak and thin and, because of the impoverished blood supply, there is pallor and shivering. Sometimes
the chest muscles are so constricted there is a sensation of
smothering, relieved by deep breathing and sighs. Dull-wittedness is common and there is an irresistible urge to sleep.
These physical retreats are the outer vestments of the conscious mind's attempt to stop time, delaying the moment
when the loss must be faced.

Jean-Paul Sartre has a theory that all emotions are attempts
to change the world. The fainting induced by fear, for
example, is a device to avoid the knowledge of danger. By
"lowering the flame of life to a pinpoint," Sartre says the
grieving achieve a state of non-living in which they don't
have to begin reorganizing their lives.

Nature is inclined to be impatient of the vacuum in
which the melancholy loiter. Eventually appetite returns

imperiously and then routine begins to absorb attention. Finally even curiosity is restored and the body, dragging its heart a little, starts living again.

Studies of those who mourn unreasonably long have some striking features. In many cases the despondency that goes on and on for months, growing worse until there may even be suicide attempts, is the mark of self-grieving. The mourner expressed himself through the identity of the lost person and had little else in his own life that seemed workable. The death then removed two people, leaving the shell of one of them. People whose sense of self-value is so flimsy that only one prop maintains them are exposing themselves to a crippling sorrow. They are depending perhaps on a pet dog, that can be killed by a car; or a mate, whose days are not infinite; or on a job of preening importance which has come to signify the summation of their dignity, but is subject to ruthless change. Investigations of the suicides that followed the 1929 stock market crash revealed that the men who killed themselves drew little or no pride from their families, friendships and self-evaluation, but only from their money. With the wealth gone, they were then totally bankrupt.

Mourning is also prolonged when guilt is involved and, since no human relationship is without blemish, guilt is always a factor in depression. In cases where there is a quantity of hatred beneath the love, the tone of the ensuing grief is one of remorse, a sticky substance that wears off very slowly.

Some adults are inconsolable at the death of their elderly parents because they recognize that their childhood has also died. The protection and indulgences of the parent-child relationship have been extended, an incongruous canopy, over balding men and women with sagging breasts. They weep because they now must be responsible, self-reliant adults, and feel alone.

Many believe that lifelong wakes, such as Queen Victoria's over Albert or Dickens' Miss Havisham's over being jilted, are glorious embracements of an appropriate excuse for a long

soak in misery or irascibility. It is an opportunity to embrace
a mood that has been concealed and there naturally is re-
luctance to recover. Especially in cases of a long-term underlying depression, bereavement is likely to be regarded as
permission to give up the fight and be melancholy openly
and forever.

Oddly, the Christian religion, though devised by Christ to
be based squarely on love, is rarely interpreted so as to be
of any use to the depressed. It often has the opposite effect
since its dogma curiously duplicates the exact conditions
which foster melancholia: the enchantment at first of the
Garden of Eden, then the abrupt expulsion and innocence
informed that it is sinful, degraded and must everlastingly
atone. The branches of the faith that take their Bible literally
are characterized by the self-loathing and guilt of their ad-
herents and the deep-seated depression which they are
obliged to mask with masochistic fortitude.

Long-term depression is an aging emotion. Blood vessels
become constricted and the heart rate slows, so that even
grieving infants have dry withered skin. The poor flow of
blood results in headaches, constipation, unending tiredness,
sleeplessness, backache, poor ability to concentrate or remember, giddiness and sour digestion. The distinguished
Danish physiologist Carl Lange commented, "There can be
little doubt that continuous sorrow may have an atrophying
effect upon the internal organs. Sorrowful persons have the
appearance of senility."

Depression eventually produces a variety of real illnesses,
among them asthma, colitis, diabetes and tuberculosis. The
U.S. psychiatrist Karl Menninger observed about the last, "It
is, after all, a graceful way to destroy oneself."

Many depressed people take a short cut. There is a rec-
ognizable suicide every few minutes in North America; the
real total is concealed in motor accident statistics, drownings,
deaths believed caused by carelessness or illness. Young
mothers who feel in a suicidal mood pose a particular problem, because they are likely to murder their children first,

regarding them—as neurotic mothers usually do—as extensions of themselves.

Dramatic suicides have a hypnotic effect on those who have been mulling over methods. A suicide in the Niagara Falls, for instance, promptly causes a small epidemic of jumping into the Niagara River. A Japanese girl who leaped into a volcano in 1933 received a great deal of newspaper attention. The following year the volcano was a favorite tourist attraction; three hundred and fifty people subsequently committed suicide there and a thousand more were prevented from doing so.

Men are more likely to commit suicide than are women, and tend to use irreversible techniques, such as a gun to the temple or stepping out of a fiftieth-story window. Women often hope to be prevented from killing themselves and prefer such remediable methods as poisons and wrist-cutting. The incidence of male suicides between the ages of twenty-five and thirty-four is nineteen per hundred thousand of population; for women, eight per hundred thousand. In their late sixties and early seventies men suicide at the rate of sixty-two per hundred thousand, while the female rate is unchanged at eight.

"By simple mathematics," suggested Lillian E. Smith and Paula Snelling, "the sex that has to spend nine months in the begetting of each human being would have less time to devote to the service of death, were it equally inclined, than has the sex of whom nine minutes are required."

All moods of depression start with unusual snappishness and inexplicable fatigue. The self-dislike of the person is so bitter it has a taste in the mouth. Despite the tiredness, sleeping is difficult. The victim usually wakens hours before dawn and reviews his failures, enlarging them grotesquely and despising his successes. At this stage, the mood usually lightens as the day progresses and it switches off entirely during some absorbing work, or a movie, or a conversation.

Often melancholia wears off in a few weeks, as inexplicably as it came. If it doesn't, the physical complaints begin:

inability to concentrate, headaches, nausea, aching muscles, lack of sexual potency and interest, menstrual difficulties, constipation, periodic blotchiness of face and neck, a dry mouth, weight loss because food is repulsive, pallor, chilly hands and feet. It is nearly impossible to work because the brain is dazed; distractions no longer distract. Tolerance of stress is almost wiped out—criticism, unintentional snubs, extra duties and unpleasant situations all provoke fury and increase hopelessness. Suicide is alluring and the fears of poverty, illness and some nameless disaster dominate the conscious mind. The soul is sickened with guilt and self-condemnation.

It is time to see a doctor. Depression is the easiest of all mankind's emotional malfunctions to treat. Pills, shock and therapy make short work of melancholia; one former model who attempted suicide on Christmas Day and awoke to find herself certified insane in a mental hospital was back at work six weeks later, somewhat shaky but able to cope with her problems.

A feeling of inability to maintain a role, either of the person who lives in the imagination or of the person that society has come to expect, is the very heart of melancholia. By exaggerating the bleakness and coldness of the world, the individual excuses himself from combat; he is too sensitive, too frail, too aware to endure cruelty and injustice. Sartre comments: "The emotion of sadness is the magical play-acting of impotence." The melancholy person gets moving again by simultaneously recognizing that all humans are frail and that he isn't as overmatched as he thought.

The recovery from sorrow over a loss is similiar. The individual is convinced he cannot continue alone, and then gradually discovers that he can. The Chinese have a story about a woman who asked Buddha to restore her dead child. He agreed, if in return she would bring him some grains of mustard seed from a plant growing in the garden of a home to which death had never come. The woman returned to Buddha empty-handed and chastened.

A United States clergyman, Charles Francis Potter, wrote about his parish in Edmonton during the First World War. The Canadian city had sent more than a thousand members of the Princess Pat Regiment to the front and a few weeks later only sixty-five were alive. Mr. Potter found a widow in his congregation who had, in his words, "triumphed over her grief" and he sent the next widow who came to him to visit her. Eventually he had a group of stalwart women who were capable of consoling others and one another.

Cicero said, "There is no grief which time does not lessen and soften." It's true, except in cases where the mourning is for the death of one's own self-esteem. Such sadness goes on and on. Anton Chekhov, the Russian playwright and humanitarian who suffered from depression all his life, wore a pendant on his watch chain inscribed, "For the lonely man, the desert is everywhere."

Profound blues are destructive and must be eased if existence is to have any point. It once was assumed that no man could recover from the early loss of his self-respect, but modern psychology has found that this isn't true. Mature adults have emerged from years of heavy depression. They achieve stability by abandoning the false techniques—popularity, praise, success—and concentrating on the subtle, winning ways of inner honesty, sympathy, forgiveness of themselves, consideration and tact for others. It is uphill work, the most private variety of courage, but ultimately it provides a victory of real splendor.

The philosopher Immanuel Kant was one of many who believed that a first-hand knowledge of melancholy is a requisite of maturity. A man who has known sadness, he said, "values himself and regards every human being as a creature who merits respect."

The Soviet poet, Yevgeny Yevtushenko, has added, "People who see danger in sadness are themselves immensely dangerous to mankind. Artificial optimism doesn't make people advance; it makes them mark time. A clean, honest, unsentimental melancholy, for all its air of helplessness, urges us forward, creating with its fragile hands the greatest spiritual treasures of mankind."

CHAPTER NINE

The Unmerry Christmas Emotions

Christmas frequently is an emotional catastrophe. The "merry Christmas" season, joy-to-the-world days, happy Chanukah time of the year bring many people to the brink of suicide, divorce and murder. The newspapers are filled with violence and there is argument under the mistletoe.

It is a paradox that has been intriguing psychiatrists for half a century, but few people are aware that a dread of December isn't singular and out of key but timeless and nearly universal.

The truth is few people get through the gala holidays without feeling decidedly upset at one time or another. With some it is only an aesthetic flinching from all the insistent jolliness. Others, particularly those suspended in the middle years between taskless childhood and self-indulgent old age, are harassed and frightened by the cheerless shopping, wrapping, mailing, cooking and debts. There is a growing disgust that what was intended to be a gentle religious festival has been hoked out of shape by the vandalism of vendors.

Quite a number of people have an old grudge against Christmas, which regularly renews the disappointment, suffering or loneliness of some childhood Christmases. A proportion of these have what amounts to an annual breakdown at Christmas—doctors call it the holiday syndrome or Christmas neurosis. The main symptoms are depression and anger; they don't always show, since ho-ho heartiness seems to be obligatory.

These people are gloomy *because* of the idealized warmth and sweetness of the season, not in spite of it. Since they don't experience the elation and good will that seems to abound, their inner desolation can only be viewed as a personal failure. Lacking the spirit of friendliness that pervades others, they mark themselves down as insufficient human beings.

Many can bask in Christmas as children do, frankly relishing the food and drink treats, the excitement of clandestine gift hiding, the giddiness of parties and colored lights. It's a mass regression to childhood, a safe self-indulgence that can be atoned for neatly by New Year's resolutions and taking down the decorations.

But even those with a benign childhood to regress into have flickers of doubt about Christmas. Carol singing can grow tedious, week after week. Outdoor decorations have become sharply competitive and are irksome to arrange. Gift-shopping is exhaustion and irritation in a pure form. The relatives gather, and are not always a happy sight.

An increasing proportion of adults deliberately plan to be away from home for Christmas in order to avoid the seasonal pressures, only to find themselves sourly marking the oddity of Christmas lights in a palm tree or the revolting folksiness of strangers in a ski lodge, while Christmas cards from people they forgot pursue them.

"Not being joyous during the Christmas season is much more common than most of us realize," observed a report by four psychiatrists at the University of Utah, who intensively studied the psychological complaints at yuletide and found them profuse.

Dismay, to a mild degree at least, is total. Sociologists have noted that ordinary conversations during the pre-Christmas rush are rarely luminous with good will. Women swap stories of their weariness, their shopping mishaps, the greediness of their get; men are vastly uneasy over the mounting expenses and their tendency to drink too much. "There are few spontaneous exclamations about how wonderful it all is," commented a distinguished Montreal psychiatrist, Dr. Alastair MacLeod. "There seems to be a great deal of hostility and anger over being impelled into something distasteful."

The tender concepts of the season, in the Christian religion the simplicity of a baby Saviour and in Judaism the candle-light memorial to freedom, are hard to discern under the smothering of carnival tensions. Instead of the gain in tranquillity expected, there is a steep loss.

One of the world's best-known psychoanalysts, Dr. Ernest Jones, once wrote that Christmas represents psychologically "the ideal of resolving all family discord in happy reunion." It's too fragile an ideal to survive, since distance, divorce and death can make it impossible and old grievances within the family somehow manage to become fresh, raw wounds again at Christmas.

The disappointment when the dream is foiled by the perversity of fate or the immortality of quarrels is acute. Christmas becomes a time of ready rage. The suicide rate climbs; murders, fist fights, mutilating insults, heavy drinking and sullen moods are typical of the season; policemen work around the clock.

The incongruous miseries of Christmas are a stronger brew of the same discontent that undermines many vacations and even idle Sunday afternoons. Psychiatrists have observed that many people are disillusioned by their holidays. They go through the motions of enthusiasm and a tiring show of gaiety, but inwardly they are dismal and homesick. It is partly because of their unrealistic hope for magic: a wonderful, happy time; it is also due to the flimsiness of most personalities—they are maintained by the familiarity of routine and collapse in strange surroundings.

The U.S. psychoanalyst J. P. Cattell describes what he calls the holiday syndrome as being most severe during the month before Christmas and until a few days after New Year's. In 1954 he reported to the American Psychoanalytic Association that the syndrome is characterized by the "presence of diffuse anxiety, numerous regressive phenomena including marked feelings of helplessness, possessiveness and increased irritability, nostalgic or bitter rumination about holiday experiences of youth, depressive effect and a wish for magical resolution of problems."

Many people bear with year-long humiliations and sadness but cannot avoid the silly hope that Christmas morning will cure it all. The season brings forth an inner child, a loitering Peter Pan who wants cuddling and gets instead a hatful of bills. It seems appropriate to be pampered at Christmas, but an impersonal stampede trampels quietness to death. The discovery that Christmas is an expensive cheat, with only a flash or two of the luster promised, creates a disillusionment that silver bells can only mock.

Some people have a clear idea of what is wrong with Christmas for them. One novelist, for instance, was deserted by his wife at Christmas and a television personality buried his only daughter a few days after she had helped him decorate a Christmas tree. Neither could tolerate holly and tinsel stars afterwards. A young mother of three whose critical in-laws visited for six weeks every Christmas eventually detested the entire season. An engineer felt a chill every Christmas that was the residue of his mother's icy insistence that he open his gifts alone in his room and stay there until dinner. A man who was raised in an orphanage was depressed every Christmas because his children never seemed grateful enough for his bounty.

The North American accent on gift exchanging at Christmas is believed to account for much of the seasonal blues.

To a child's mind—and many an adult's as well—the quantity and quality of gifts received is the tangible evidence of how much he is loved. Friends who receive more and better gifts are envied because they must be valued more. A brother or sister getting a more lavish present is a disaster. For this reason, even mature people feel a droop in spirits as the last gift is unwrapped, while young children are inclined to protest violently.

The emotional involvement in gift giving is such that people who are unable to love their families because of their own inadequacies tend to give luxurious presents. By going into debt for copious gifts, they punish themselves satisfyingly and their consciences are calmed for awhile.

Christmas accordingly can be an economic calamity. Instead of sugar plums, many heads are filled with a dance of creditors while panic in its tutu waits in the wings. The financial demands of the gifts, tips to tradesmen, extra food and drink, cards and stamps, Christmas trees and extension cords, all crumple the sense of safety many find in a working budget. The breadwinner knows naked horror, as his children pipe "Silent Night."

Many are reminded by the hysteria of Christmas of the potlatch customs of some West Coast Indians, who destroy their enemies by loading them with gifts and food. The guests of honor are required to return the ceremony with even more sumptuous gifts and food, thus wrecking their resources if they comply or plunging them into disgrace if they don't. Christmas gift giving similarly is becoming a persecution for many people: there is a mutually ruinous trend on this continent to give back a slightly better gift than was received.

But worry over debt and disgrace is only part of the disharmony of Christmas. Some scientists, notably Dr. Jones, suspect that a primitive identification with the sun affects all mankind, so that the waning of the winter sun rekindles the primitive fear that human powers are weakening as well.

Some of the responsibility for Christmas depression must

then lie with the early Christians who chose December 25 as Christ's birthday because this was the date of the most widely celebrated of pagan festivals and therefore eased conversion. Ardent sun-worshipers in man's early history believed that the winter solstice, the shortest day of the year, was the date on which the old sun died and a new one was born. They therefore celebrated giddily, with plentiful food and drink, in their best attire, fires lit to support the burgeoning young sun. The Romans ornamented their homes with wreaths and exchanged gifts and hospitality. The Druids gathered mistletoe and the Saxons holly and ivy.

More than three hundred years after the death of Christ, many of the new church's followers were distressed that Jesus was still regarded as a minor figure, of negligible importance next to his father. To elevate his reputation, they decided to mark his birth date with a festival. The actual date is debatable (most scholars place it in the spring) so the ancient Christians tried several dates before settling on the day of the feast to the sun, deemed appropriate since it already celebrated a birth.

It was a technique of the time to winnow non-believers into Christianity by duplicating their favorite holidays. The Feast of Epiphany, for instance, takes place on the day that Egyptians used to mark the virgin birth of their god Aeon. The festival of the goddess Diana was replaced with the Assumption of the Virgin and the Celtic feast of the dead became All Souls' Day. Occasionally Christians revolt against the bawdy beginnings of their most sacred days: an act of English Parliament in 1644 abolished Christmas as "a heathen festival" but the law proved so unpopular that the holiday was reinstated promptly when Charles II took the throne.

Similarly, the Jewish ceremonial lighting of candles during Chanukah bears the imprint of pagan sun-worshiping. The eight days of Chanukah have many points of resemblance to the Roman Saturnalia, also a festival of good will and rejoicing which was originally observed on December 19 and later extended so that it lasted seven days. Chanukah, the happiest of all Jewish ceremonial days, celebrates the victory of a Jewish tribe, the Maccabees, in history's first war of principle.

The selection of deep, dark, cold winter for festivities sets up a conflict that adds to the seasonal muddle of emotions. All by themselves, days of brief sunshine can induce melancholy. So does the imminence of the year's end—the dying of time, years running out, potency running out, life running out.

In addition to these despondent thoughts, North American Jews often find Chanukah a time of painful yielding. Their holiday is less spectacular than the gaudy Christian Christmas and the comparison is distressing to their children. To offset this, some Jewish parents decorate a tree—wryly calling it a Chanukah bush—and put presents beneath it. These concessions shame the devout, who are shocked at the hypocrisy, and also trouble the parents who practice them because the suggestion of disloyalty is unavoidable.

But the deepest and most serious depressions of the season, some of them dipping into mental illness, are those which are the legacy of a childhood jealousy. Some doctors have discovered that Christians under psychoanalysis will reveal an unconscious and corrosive envy of the infant Christ, who receives homage, love and attention and cannot be competed against. Adults who long for the mothering they missed feel a stab they dare not acknowledge at reproductions of the nativity scene, with a tender and adoring Mary bent over her baby.

Christmas in fact celebrates world-wide love for an infant, while it is the lot of many modern babies to have very little of it. The disparity is particularly galling to the unloved at Christmas. The humbug of the season for them is not the commercialism but the reminder of their own insufficient mothering.

The childishness of the merrymaking associated with Christmas lulls some people into a suspension of reality. They give themselves an orgy of candy and late nights and a good time, at the expense of their normal standards. Not many can regress into thoughtless, consequenceless childhood and still keep alert the internal watchman who knows from experience that pipers have the strongest union in the world and always get their pay. The pull between the intoxicant of self-indulgence and wisdom that accrues from remorse is never so weighted on the side of abandon as during those darkest days of winter in late December.

The Christmas-Chanukah observances, however, cannot in themselves impose an untypical mood, but they may release the stranger within every man. The thumb of conscience is able to squelch a good deal of lunacy, cupidity and venom during ordinary days and ordinary tasks, but at holiday time the conscience can be bought off with excuses and malice pops out, and envy, and fury, and the realization of loneliness. One of the side-effects is an aroused sexual appetite and an interest in aberration.

Sándor Ferenczi, the brilliant Hungarian psychoanalyst, was interested in the phenomenon of holiday depression. He noted that the loosening of external and internal restrictions is frightening to many people, causing them to feel anxious, despondent, restive and ill. The period surrounding Chanukah, Christmas and New Year's Day is the annual spree of the personality, during which spontaneity and exuberance are encouraged. As a result it can exert a most disastrous effect on people who are sure of themselves only when they are being ruled by routine.

Dr. Jules Eisenbud, a New York psychoanalyst, observed in a paper, "Negative Reactions to Christmas," that the season permits "social sanction to forms of enjoyment which at other times must be held to a judicious minimum." Another psychoanalyst, Dr. L. Bruce Boyer, added, "It is to be expected that the degree of neurotic response to such an intense holiday release would be frequent and severe."

Psychiatrists are collecting an interesting dossier of holiday syndrome case histories. One of them describes a woman

engineer who was an exhibitionist and harshly aggressive because she constantly was convinced that she wasn't wanted.
Christmas was a special hell time for her. "I used to feel
that if I didn't find something wonderful that Christmas, I'd
find it another," she told her doctor. The "something wonderful" was a talisman, some demonstration of love that
could penetrate her skepticism. Each Christmas she became
more devastated by its absence.

Another woman expressed hatred of her preferred brother
regularly every Christmas, a depth of malevolence that never
failed to surprise and upset her. A psychiatrist discovered that
her recollection of the favoritism shown her brother was always refreshed at Christmas, a time when her parents gave
him elaborate, expensive gifts and gave her meager things.

A department-store buyer who also grew up with a much
favored brother became ruthless in her business relationships
with men during the Christmas season and twice was fired
because of it. Her doctor found that she once had asked Santa
Claus to turn her into a boy so her parents would like her
better. The collapse of her hope left her with an annual
vendetta against the masculine sex.

A salesman who loathed Christmas intensely was able to
trace it to an event that occurred when he was nine years old.
He discovered a new bicycle hidden behind his house. Since
he had been begging his parents for a bike, he assumed that
he had stumbled on his Christmas gift and ecstatically
awaited December 25. The bicycle that morning went to his
handsomer and more clever brother. The man never forgave
Christmas for the heartbreak he endured; the pangs returned
vividly every season.

A strongly religious woman went to a psychiatrist in horror
when she realized that every Christmas she was hating Christ
more and more. She was blaming the infant, it turned out,
for her own emotionally barren childhood. A beautiful young
girl began to quarrel hotly with her fiancé at Christmas. The
cause was traced to the fact that Christmas had been the
time when she felt most bitterly deprived of her father, who

had deserted the family when she was small. Christmas served to remind her that men could be deceitful, that they had power to hurt women.

The Utah psychiatrists studied the case of a man who was so wretched in his home town at Christmas that he annually fled to a nudist camp, the farthest extreme from normal yuletide that he could invent. A father, otherwise a responsible citizen, passed bad checks every Christmas. Another, who always delighted his family with his thoughtfulness on their birthdays and anniversaries, flatly refused to buy anyone a Christmas gift at all. A divorcée was able to endure her isolation every other month but December—Christmas had been sentimental in her family. She regularly wept throughout the entire day and broke out in hives.

Some people for whom Christmas has no especially unpleasant associations nevertheless detest the season. In some cases, it is because the strain of household upheaval is too much for the orderliness of their natures. Their homes seem unfamiliar, decked out with once-a-year ornaments and shifted furniture and they accordingly feel disturbed and vaguely worried. Children frequently become ill at Christmas, succumbing gladly to whatever infection they can pick up rather than face the uneven mealtimes and extra visitors.

Whatever causes it—lack of sunshine, childhood jealousy, confusion, old wounds, or apprehensions because the lid is off—the holiday syndrome is now attracting the medical attention it deserves. The chief benefit so far is that many people are enormously relieved to find that they are not unsociable freaks because they dread Christmas but rather are being quite normal.

As a result of the new acceptance of anti-Christmas spirit, many families have exchanged techniques for making the season more tolerable. Some have stopped sending out Christmas cards, making a straight donation of the money saved to UNICEF, or retarded or crippled children, or CARE packages. It takes a few years to complete the job, but eventually they notify all their relatives, friends and acquaintances that they no longer send cards.

A musician with the Toronto Symphony Orchestra had a family conference one autumn and it was agreed that each person would receive only one gift at Christmas—the resultant savings would go to impoverished families in Europe. A Fredericton, New Brunswick, industrialist gave his wife an unusual gift in 1963: he adopted an eleven-year-old Korean boy through the Foster Parents' Plan.

On that same Christmas, a Canadian priest, Father Murray Abraham, wrote a powerful poem, printed in the *Canadian Messenger of the Sacred Heart*. He interspersed his observations between the lines of one of Pope John XXIII's pronouncements. Called "Pacem in Terris," it contained in part:

"Every human being has the right to life."
    I see twins born in Singell,
    tiny, brown, Nepali twins,
    cradled in the coarse, cracked grimy hands
       of a coolie woman,
    laid on a blanket crawling with filth,
    laid on a mud floor, clammy and cold, doomed to death
    they lie there panting their first, precious breath.

"Every human being has the right to physical integrity."
    I see beggars swarming around me like flies
    in station after station across sweating India,
    clutching at my arm, grovelling before me
    twisted limbs, sightless eyes, rotting bodies,
       stinking sores.
    My heart aches; my stomach is sick!

"Every human being has the right to security whenever he is deprived of the means of subsistence as a result of circumstances beyond his control."
    I see a crowd of coolies, standing in the
       cement shed,
    watching the monsoon rain with blank, bitter eyes,
    rain—hour after hour after hour,

every hour of rain, an hour less pay, an
    hour more hunger.
It is raining pain.
. . . Oh God! the sights I have seen! the sounds I
    have heard!
And in the West
    the sights I have seen? the sounds I have heard?

Merry Christmas!
    I see stores gaudy with gifts, crammed with
        crowds
    packed with the nerve-racking noise, the
        clatter, the chatter, the clang
        of cash-registers, the clickety-
        clack of toys
    and underneath and above and in and through and
        around it all a song: beautiful
        and blasphemous
    "Silent Night, Holy Night; All is calm, all
        is bright."

Merry Christmas!
    I see the words of Time (or is it Eternity?)
        of Life (or is it Death?)
    "Four billion dollars spent. . . ."
    For one Christmas day
    For two hundred million overfed Americans,
    more than all the help given over ten years
    for four hundred million underfed Indians. O
        God! O God!

Gentle John, Shepherd John,
    Call us with your shepherd's voice.
    Lead us out of mockery, out of mean,
        meaningless mockery.
    Lead us away from the Christmas tree.
    Lead us back to the Christmas cave.
    Christmas is God born poor,
    homeless,
    cold,
    rejected,
    If we have gifts to give, teach us to
        give to the poor,

the homeless,
the cold,
the rejected.
Christ is the starving beggar on the
    streets of Calcutta.
Christ is the weeping widow in the slums
    of Rio de Janeiro.
Christ is the child crying, crying in
    the hovels of Cairo.
Lead us back to Christ, gentle shepherd
    John.
Christ needs us.
He brought peace to us, let us now bring
    peace to him.
"Pacem in Terris." Amen. Amen.

Father Abraham's protest has millions of sympathizers of every faith. In a hungry world, the North American Christmas-Chanukah has become indecent. Men and women distressed by the fever and acceleration and false camaraderie of the season have been in composed retreat these past few years. They have soothed themselves by forgiving the injustices of Christmases Past and expecting no miracles in Christmases Future. There is a trend toward more gentle family celebrations, with simpler trimmings and truer warmth. They find that with the hustle and greed removed, the pagan season has worth again: a sense of holiness returns, and peace, and even joy.

CHAPTER TEN

Guilt Is Usually a Fool

For North Americans, this is the age of guilt. Men feel guilty because they are not masculine enough and women because they are not feminine enough. People feel guilty if they are poor and they feel guilty if they are rich. The colored feel guilty because they have made the inexcusable mistake of being born black, and whites feel guilty because they are bigoted. Men feel guilty because they compromise their ideals, because they can't love their families, because they are fearful; women feel guilty because they are strident, because they can't find happiness, because they envy. Children feel guilty because they rarely meet the expectations of their parents.

Yet guilt is a venal cretin, the greatest cheat of all the elements that make up the human personality. A gossip who does her best to see that sinners get their just desserts feels guilty only if her housework is undone. Executives take credit for work done by others but feel guilty if they forget a birthday. Murderers hate to be unkempt; swindlers are kind to their mothers; corrupted politicians attend orphans picnics; torturers keep neat closets.

On the other hand, people who lead blameless lives may suffer excruciating guilt over an erotic dream. A devout person will experience agony if he has a flash of hatred he can't justify. Perfectionists are tormented all the time by guilt, since they can never be truly perfect.

Yet this arch-fool, guilt, is indispensable to the development of decency. As Julian Huxley phrased it, guilt is the embryonic notochord which can grow into a backbone called ethics. Without a sense of guilt, mankind would be as animals are: neither moral nor immoral, but simply non-moral. Most people, unhappily for all, don't develop their guilt all the way to wisdom and integrity; their backbones are slightly floppy, and bend to mad winds.

Guilt can only begin in a human baby who cares about someone he sees regularly. The condition for the birth of guilt is the disapproval of someone the infant has come to admire. This is why children who as babies were handed from foster home to foster home, or from housekeeper to housekeeper, or were raised in short-staffed institutions tend to have a conscience that operates on a minimal level or is absent altogether. The baby must like some adult very much in order to feel distressed when he offends, or when he has had the temerity to loath the adult for a few minutes.

Guilt grows by leaps in two-year-olds, who are always being shouted at by mothers and who are more openly angry at their mothers than they will ever dare be again. Three-year-olds have learned the knack of avoiding conflict: they give themselves orders, sometimes aloud and in the tone their mothers use. This is the sound of a conscience being born—someone else's concept of right and wrong. A six-year-old's conscience has some added elements, the right and wrong as defined by his school and the games he plays. It never occurs to a small child that adults he likes can ever be wrong, and so every clash with them produces guilt in the child. Eventually he will suffer guilt even if he isn't discovered in what has been defined as wrongdoing; his brand-new conscience sees to it that he is punished.

Psychologists call this stage of moral development an authoritarian conscience, and note that millions of adults never mature beyond it. They continue to accept the values of the community in which they live, no matter how cruel or senseless their resultant behavior may be. Their consciences are easy when they follow the leader, and prickle only when they digress. The authoritarian consciences of many Germans lead them to accept the genocide of the Jews as virtuous.

The ideal circumstances for crippling a conscience at the authoritarian level are parents who are cool, rigid and right. They tolerate no disobedience or criticism and effectively crush the child's ability to be spontaneous, to originate himself. Mistakes are severely punished and the child grows up to be an adult with a heavy sense of guilt over trivia such as untidiness or fundamentals such as divergent opinions. To preserve his sanity, he adopts whatever moral code is most popular and doesn't dare to doubt.

The psychotherapist Otto Rank calls the owner of such a strait-jacket conscience the "average man." By making no effort to be an individual, he avoids the conflicts that stir up guilt. He conforms to his society in order to spare himself growth pains. "It represents the first and easiest solution of the problem set by birth," observes Dr. Rank coldly.

"A good conscience, from an authoritarian point of view, depends on blind submission, mitigated by trust in the love of the superior," noted writer-psychoanalyst Erich Fromm. "It is a withdrawal from the constructive love of self and from human responsibility for the destiny of the race."

Geography and religion are factors in this mangling of a human conscience. The Protestant religion, for instance, particularly those sin-and-damnation versions of it, instill copious guilt in their followers without providing the outlet of the confessional. John Calvin and Martin Luther, who founded two of the most punitive branches of Protestantism, were both abused mercilessly as children.

In North America, the middle class is most guilt-prone,

since it tends to bow unquestioningly to the household gods of uniformity, reliability and popularity. These are the people who feel guilty nearly constantly, because they can never measure up to the idealized cheerfulness and industry. The Manus tribe of the Admiralty Islands, who are almost the personal property of anthropologist Margaret Mead, also raises its children with strict puritanical codes and goals. Dr. Mead describes them as "stone-age people with modern guilt," the consequence of their prudishness, hysterical sex taboos and anxiety to be a success, by Manus terms.

The German race also raises its children adamantly, praising them for the virtue of obedience to authority and punishing them severely for the sin of disobedience. It results in a citizenry of emphatic sheep; the high point of a German's lifetime occurs in his youth, when he stages a temporary, jubilant revolt. Similarly, the British upper class is thwarted from the fluidity of mature personality by means of the nanny and public school system, which instills artificial control and a ten-ton stone of guilt.

The morality of parents is a contagion, which when it is accompanied by the assumption that it is faultless can lead to a permanently ill conscience. Jean Piaget, of Geneva University, studied the thought processes of young children and discovered that they mimic ethics. Parents who conceive of child-raising as a process of eternal vigilance against the wickedness of children will almost certainly raise an untrusting tyrant. If parents prize material possessions, the child's emerging conscience will wound him when he fails a public test. If the parents admire bland deportment, the child will be horrified by his own anger. If they equate virtue with denial, the child suffers from eating a chocolate bar.

In immature people, the conscience is a colossally inefficient instrument for detecting right and wrong. John Dewey, the United States philosopher and educator, considered it highly indicative of the maturity of a family to discover how the parents answered the question, "Why should I tell the truth?" Some reply flatly that lying is a sin and that's that; some explain that liars are unpopular; some that the result is certain exposure and ridicule; a few that society would break down if people couldn't rely on one another.

"To a marked degree, culture, class membership and their respective prejudices mold both conscience and conduct," the renowned United States psychologist Gordon W. Allport stated in his 1955 Terry lectures at Yale. "Early fixations in character often leave infantile traces that bind the mind in such a way that democratic relationships in adult life are impossible."

Dr. Allport noted three stages in the development of a human conscience. The first one is when external sanctions rule, a situation accepted wholly by babies and adults with criminal inclinations. The conscience responds to a very simple credo: everything which escapes detection is good and everything that is caught is wrong.

The second stage is an internal duplication of these external sanctions, so that rules are obeyed even when rule-makers are absent. The conscience directs behavior, incorporating importantly the dicta of mother, father, clergy, police, teachers and society—*to the extent that the parents, and consequently the child, respect those authorities.* This complicated, discordant mishmash becomes the conscience of a ten-year-old child, one which most adults are careful to preserve all their lives, as if it were a personal communication from the Mount.

It is pure chaos. Herbert W. Schneider, a philosopher and theologian at Columbia University for many years, commented sadly, "People sometimes have a very moral attitude about stealing, but an immoral one about war, politics or justice."

The highest development of the human conscience, Dr. Allport's third stage, is the one termed humanistic, when the adult is self-guided according to his own "experiences of preference and self-respect." Humanistic ethics require social regulations, Dr. Fromm explains, "but the distinction is that the authority behind them resides in man himself." The person has taken the ultimate step: he is responsible to himself for himself.

It's a rare state. Just as no autopsy has yet unskinned a perfectly formed human being—and indeed regularly uncover defects that astonish doctors, who cannot imagine how the individual maintained a normal life—no one is perfectly mature emotionally. Guilt stands damned among the deforming aspects of man's personality because it is present in every neurosis.

Karen Horney, writer and psychoanalyst, states, "In the manifest picture of neuroses, guilt feelings seem to play a paramount role. In some neuroses these feelings are expressed openly and abundantly; in others they are more disguised, but their presence is suggested by behavior, attitudes and ways of thinking and reacting."

The great neurotic fear is of being found out, exposed as a fake. It is the handiwork of guilt which gives a sense of unworthiness, of inner ugliness, of being undeserving of love or respect. There is a discrepancy between the personality being presented to the world, a friendly and capable thing, and the real person inside, sordid and disgusting. It is as though a filthy fortress was being manned by a gala show, impressive enough to win momentary victory but certain to be revealed as a sham army. Guilt is lonelier than loneliness and more frightening than fear.

Dr. Horney points out that some people who suffer from guilt show it blatantly. They assume the blame instantly, insist that mishaps are always their fault, change their minds whenever they encounter disagreement. They detest themselves, conjuring up fantasies that exaggerate their minor shortcomings but managing to justify by elaborate convolutions their genuine failings. They actually feel better and behave more coherently during a disaster; playing the martyr suits their souls perfectly.

As psychiatrists have discovered, people rather admire guilt in themselves and are reluctant to give it up, believing it a sign of superior sensitivity not shared by peasants. Dr. Horney is among the many therapists who have come to believe that guilt complexes don't rest on a conviction of failure so much as egoism as blatant and narcissistic as a baby's. The guilt-ridden person is affronted if friends weary of his hand-wring-ing and agree with him that he is faulty; he is a great admirer, he claims, of constructive criticism but all criticism aimed at him seems to fall into another category; he isn't worth bother-ing about, he insists, but his protests wring from others con-tinuous reassurances, praise and attention.

Others with too much guilt are more subtle. Some are with-drawn, suspicious and irritated by personal questions, secretive about themselves. One woman, asked by an acquaintance if she planned to marry, replied stonily, "I never even tell people if I *am* married." It's a ploy to avoid exposure, which might invite rejection or malice.

Some are ferociously "loving," so overwhelmingly tending of their victims that escape or protests would seem to be unreasonable. Many highly guilt-laden people put out perfec-tion, relentlessly fulfilling obligations—many of them self-in-vented—and being Samaritans in order to build up a case against censure. Still others take the tactic of helplessness, becoming poor in health or even crippled so that no one but a villain would dare to be unkind. A variation of this technique is excessive childishness: men and women whose whimsy it is to be playfully and amusingly baffled by budgets, routine and responsibilities. Being enchantingly unable to cope, they withdraw from the field, having one huge, general failure on their consciences rather than a multitude of specific lapses.

Over-guilt is but one dysfunction of the conscience—lack of guilt is the other. People with infantile consciences break rules, behave willfully and upon impulse. Experience teaches them nothing but to be more careful next time in order to avoid being discovered. These people are a nuisance to society and a horror to their families but are no trouble at all to them-selves. Genially amoral or edgy with hatred, their existence is a series of excuses, evasions and acts of contempt. Their mood swings are sudden, violent and evanescent as a child's. They make superb mates for the over-guilty, whose masochistic need to suffer will be realized richly.

A shortage of guilt indicates a rudimentary personality, one that never embarked on the tedious, difficult, embarrassing and noble voyage of maturing. Overactive guilt indicates demi-growth, paralyzed along the way and longing to retrace its steps. There is no forward progress. While a healthy person who makes a mistake feels badly for a time but relieves his dismay by making the error good and changing his conduct, a neurotic falls into a torment of remorse, broods for weeks in actual pain, but changes nothing.

The Montreal psychiatrist-writer Karl Stern has said, "Objective guilt can be assuaged. Like debt, to which it is related, it can be paid. Neurotic guilt is insatiable. You cannot appease it. You cannot pay it off."

At the Menninger Clinic in Topeka, Kansas, patients with symptoms of guilt benefit from a practical course of treatment: punishment. Dr. Will C. Menninger explains that the sunshine and roses don't work because such a patient "will only think that you don't understand him. His troubles are burning his soul—he has to expiate in some way. We know it is a mistake to let people go on punishing themselves emotionally, so we get them to punish themselves with menial tasks." A bank president was put to work scrubbing the clay and glaze-splattered walls of the ceramics studio. A fragile old lady was given a soot-crusted pot, bought in a second-hand store, and asked to clean it. Others were given buttons to sort, or two-thousand-piece jigsaw puzzles to put together.

During the last war, an English woman became ill with guilt because she had borne an illegitimate baby. She went to a psychiatrist for treatment but grew steadily more wretched. In despair she went to a convent, where the sisters told her she was a wicked, wicked girl and put her to scrubbing floors as a penance. It was balm to her and she recovered.

Many guilt-ridden people unconsciously administer their own therapy. When they are sick at heart, women clean ovens and men tidy desks. Cleanliness, in the psychic world, seems to be a step closer to goodness. Gangsters, like Mickey Cohen, may have hand-washing phobias. (Cohen showers, shaves, shampoos and changes his clothes several times a day; so does comedian Jerry Lewis.) Many make deals with their consciences: philanderers bring home gifts to the children; ruthless businessmen support the United Appeal liberally; women who don't like sex adore babies, as a moral justification for an otherwise revolting act.

George Bernard Shaw observed astutely, "The more things a man is ashamed of, the more respectable he is."

There are other tricks to avoid guilt, the most common of which is the sophistry of "everyone does it." Income tax cheating and expense account padding are more guilt-free than is pilfering a five-cent stamp. Cribbing on examinations is catching, so is destroying reputations. In a police force where a few are known to accept bribes, many will soon be bribed. A political party whose back room deals in graft and kickbacks is going to be corrupt throughout.

The Bhagavad-Gita says, "Repeated sin impairs the judgment . . . He whose judgment is impaired sins repeatedly."

An immature conscience looks out sharply for advantage, like any hood. Meanness can be justified without much strain: "I've had it happen to me plenty of times," or "The villain had it coming to him," or "I apologized," or "I never get a fair break, what do you expect me to do?" or "I did it for the cause."

"The cause" is history's greatest gift to evil. In the name of righteousness, judges of the Inquisition put men on the rack, underground fighters dynamited human beings into fragments, the RAF flattened the wounded and refugee-packed city of Dresden, Crusaders drove their lances into Saracen babies, Jesus was crucified, Spinoza was excommunicated and Socrates ordered to drink poison. (Somewhat optimistically, Socrates said before dying, "I have been overtaken by death, but my accusers by wickedness . . . I submit to my punishment, and they to theirs.")

In the name of morality, the distribution of contraceptives is hampered, though a billion babies are born with a total legacy of hunger, filth and disease; in the name of virtue—or vengeance—abortions may not be performed safely in hospitals but instead brutally on kitchen tables, babies are put in institutions rather than in loving homes of the so-called wrong religion, children go to jail, the insane are locked in hundred-bed wards, addicts and alcoholics are punished.

While the consciences of some are kin of pious Tomás de Torquemada, others have a conscience that flails them if they leave a telephone unanswered. They can't refuse requests, even when exhausted and ill, because they labor in the Augean stable of their own disgrace and don't dare to put down the shovel. If they are in positions of authority, it is intolerable for them to fire anyone. They don't complain when exploited or cheated or insulted, because they are satisfied that they deserve no better. Occasionally a sheet of hot anger escapes them, scorching in its violence, but they expect to be forgiven because it happens so rarely.

Such a conscience, primed in the first years of life to the conviction that it inhabits a scoundrel and failure, will push a man or woman to fantastic feats of endurance and production. The lash of overwork suits their need to atone, while their hope is that success in business or the arts or society will relieve their disappointment with themselves and give peace.

"Historically," comments Margaret Mead, "this type of character structure which relies on guilt has been identified with the rise of the commercial class and invoked as a condition of the industrial revolution and the development of modern science and the machine age."

Karen Horney says that the guilty long to get rid of themselves and that exhaustion is one of the techniques intended to numb self-awareness. Other devices are inordinate amounts of sleep, addiction, sickness, insanity, promiscuity or danger. In the United States, guilt accounted for much of the $275 million spent on hard liquor in one year of the early 1960s,

$225 million on tranquilizers and $230 million on sleeping pills.

In addition to the guilt infused as a result of intolerably high standards in early life, human beings seem to inherit a subterranean stream of guilt deep in their blood. Most religions and early myths focus on guilt and the pining for forgiveness. Several writers have noted the similarities between Prometheus, who gave man fire in Greek legend, and Jesus; both endured cruel punishment as a result of helping man, and both were received back by Zeus and God. Paul may have been strongly influenced by the Greek redemption fables; the Christianity he fashioned has much in common with classic falls from grace and resurrections.

The history of guilt may be as old as the history of man. Freud wrote that guilt is "the most important problem in the evolution of culture" and anthropologist Weston La Barre notes, "Man's original sin was not so much the eating of the fruit of the tree as in climbing down from it." Mankind has since felt uneasy to be bipedal, vaguely damned because babies are born in pain and because domesticity is confining.

In particular, modern man feels guilty about sex. Men feel guilty if they desire sex too often or if they are capable too rarely; women are guilty when they are unresponsive to their mates or feel a flash of desire for a telephone lineman or the teen-ager next door; adolescents feel guilt when their bodies begin to change and men and women in the menopause years feel a matching guilt and humiliation. People experience guilt if they masturbate, guilt if they have explicit sexual dreams, guilt if they have an erotic thought about a relative.

Shame is the first cousin of guilt. Guilt is the result of a fall from the person's private expectations for himself, and shame the result of some discrepancy with society's standards. Ruth Benedict, a cultural anthropologist whose study of Japan, *The Chrysanthemum and the Sword*, is a case history of shame, states, "Shame cultures rely on external sanctions for good behavior and not, as true guilt cultures do, on an internalized conviction of sin. Shame is a reaction to other people's criticism . . . it requires an audience, or at least a man's fantasy of an audience. Guilt does not."

Japan is the world's most prominent shame culture, but the strain runs through Pacific islanders, African and Arabic races, India, the Jews and many North American Indian tribes, cultural brothers of the Japanese. The Ojibway, in particular, will commit suicide if they perform what they hold to be a shameful deed. Japanese children are imbued with the disgrace of losing face. To preserve the delicate balance that maintains their honor, the Japanese avoid competition, despair when a kindness puts them in another's debt, and vastly prefer death to ignominy. This hysterical form of shame is conditioned by the traditional Japanese style of discipline, which relies on ridicule to keep younger children in line and outright dismissal from the home of older children who disgrace themselves by being inept.

The relationship between the physical changes produced in man by shame and guilt has the same dichotomy as the psychic causes. Guilt is an interior anguish for interior reasons and keeps its symptoms to itself: the blood seems to congeal in the heavy organs, causing pounding heart, labored breathing, poor digestion and constipation. In the case of shame, which is provoked by exterior judgments, real or imagined, blood action is stepped up and the world sees a reddened face.

Scientists have found no satisfactory explanation for blushes, but they suspect it is the consequence of a physiological blunder. The rush of blood to the face is an ill-contrived attempt at concealment, it seems, reinforced by the embarrassed person's usual effort to hide his hands as well. Since clothing covers the rest of the body, the face and hands bear the brunt of the sensation of being exposed. Blushing accompanies all moments when the person feels sharply at a disadvantage—when he is clumsy, for instance, or overpraised, or wrongly accused, or has violated an etiquette. Teen-agers, whose sense of unfitness is most acute, blush more often than

adults, women more often than men and women in menopause more often than anyone in the world.

The self-judgment that leads to guilt is the bony structure
on which character hangs its flesh. If it grows straight and
true, it is the guarantee of a man's chivalry. Conscience is
crucial to the unfolding of love and integrity, without which
life is a waste. The philosopher Hegel stated, "It is the
privilege of a man to feel guilty."

Brandeis University's esteemed psychologist, Abraham
Maslow, has observed of guilt, "It is not just a symptom to
be avoided at any cost but is rather an inner guide for growth
toward the actualization of the real self, and of its potentialities."

Carl Jung called conscience the "thorn in the flesh" without which there is no progress and no ascent. The art of
living is the evolution of a sane guilt, in harmony with
abilities and capable of justice, a prod to ideals and a check
on impulsiveness.

The development of a mature conscience follows the same
order as the growth of a capacity for love. Many serious
thinkers have come to the same conclusion in recent years,
that guilt, like fear, is the opposite of love—as destructive as
hate and, perhaps, hate itself. Man must think and act his
way clear of the "crippling burden of good and evil," as Dr.
Brock Chisholm, the Canadian psychiatrist who headed the
World Health Organization for many years, has put it. Dr.
Chisholm declares, "The unnecessary and artificially imposed
inferiority, guilt and fear, commonly known as sin, produces
much of the social maladjustment and unhappiness in the
world."

Dr. Chisholm told a meeting in San Francisco in 1963
that emotional immaturity, based on consciences formed
rock-hard at six to eight years of age, constitutes the world's
greatest problem, threatening the extinction of the human
race.

The recent recognition of the devastation wrought by punitive guilt complexes has influenced many parents, among

them leading psychologists and psychiatrists, to raise their children in a spirit of permissiveness, which has been as harmful to the well-being of their offspring as a daily drubbing with cudgels. In order to avoid a tyrant of a conscience, they substitute a self-satisfied and incompetent one. Children permitted sassiness, vicious in-family fights and self-selected rules emerge into the world absolutely lost, doomed to chronic infantile restlessness.

Somewhere between the extremes is a sensible method of raising children that will give them the best chance of happiness. Dr. David Ricks, a young psychologist at Brandeis University, has been advising parents of his area to worry less about the modern stressing of insight and understanding with their children and more about setting standards "that mean enough to the parent to hold himself to them as well as hold them up to the child."

Children tend to admire goodness and to wish for it. One researcher questioned a thousand youngsters in grades six to twelve, asking them to list the qualities they admired most in others and the ones they admired least. "Honesty" topped the first list with children of every age and "dishonesty" the second.

Doing the appropriate act calls for a round of congratulations from the conscience that gives the confused child or evolving adult a breather in which to consolidate the gain. Erich Fromm views this as going with your own natural current, trusting the consequence of rightness. "Conscience is thus a reaction of ourselves to ourselves . . . that is, to become what we potentially are." It is a progression much like education, with harder and harder lessons confronting a more and more astute student. There is no graduation, but a capering exhilaration in competency.

The American poet Robert Frost once spoke of the need to discover "what you can and can't possibly stand." From this, and a stolid refusal to lie to oneself, a sound conscience can emerge and man has a chance to be immortal. Victor

Hugo was in awe of such a conscience. He wrote: "There is a spectacle grander than the ocean, and that is the conscience. There is a spectacle grander than the sky, and it is the interior of the soul."

CHAPTER ELEVEN

Anxiety Is the Useless Emotion

Anxiety begins in human beings before they are born and serves no useful purpose. In fact, it is the most destructive emotion that man can experience. In its mild state, it warps personality and behavior, making it unsuitable; severe anxiety can in a few months destroy sanity or age a digestive system twenty years; total anxiety cannot be endured for more than an instant.

Anxiety is also mysterious. It has been studied in North America more than any other emotional state of man but no one yet knows why it is aroused or how to cure it. To complicate the problem, people suffering from anxiety rarely understand what is really worrying them.

Most psychologists believe anxiety is the inevitable response to change of any kind. Two months before he is born, a baby will have an increased heartbeat if a doorbell buzzes near by, cutting through the drowsy, distant sounds he is accustomed to. During birth, babies have stepped-up heart-beats and difficulty in breathing, both of which are symptoms of anxiety in adults as well.

Four-month-old infants show what doctors stuffily term "negative effect"—a tenseness in strange situations that can probably be called anxiety. "Eight-month anxiety," which actually appears around the seventh month and lasts until the twelfth, is a frequent subject of investigation. The baby clearly is apprehensive when his mother is absent, particularly if something unusual occurs while she is away. A familiar display of early anxiety is the distress babies show with strangers, a phenomenon known to grandmothers as "making strange."

The infant's conviction that he is unprotected against a lurking and unimaginable menace is the very essence of anxiety. The danger isn't known, but its imminence is felt for no reason other than that something unfamiliar has happened. A little child in a strange crib will be uneasy, and in this agitated state he is ready to find something at which he can scream in terror: a black thread on his pillow, an insect on the wall, the flap of a blind. A grown man, dropped by a jet into a foreign city, will release the anxiety he feels in anger at the currency, the service he encounters, the bad manners of other anxious tourists.

Change always produces a sudden sense of vulnerability in both animals and man. The twentieth century, therefore, is the age of anxiety. These years are taut with mobility, innovation and transformation: migrant populations in the shadow of overkill; paranoic diplomacy and daylight violence; economic unsteadiness; fluid morality and self-defined faith; the necessity to make choices, most of them irreversible; the compulsion to matter; lovelessness, loneliness and the lack of privacy; the dislike of parents, an ancestor-destruction that dissolves the comforts of continuity; the pace of purposeless life and the presence of death.

These torments, genuine as they are, effect humans unequally. Some people are innately serene: their minds invent no disaster. Behavior scientists trace the varying levels of anxiety within individuals to early environment, which includes the pre-birth environment of the mother's body. Truly relaxed mothers produce peaceful newborn infants, who sleep deeply and are not easily startled.

Later, an infancy crowded with upheaval can put even a calm baby into an edgy state. Because the unexpected keeps happening, beyond his point of tolerance, he develops perpetual wariness. At the other extreme, a cloistered infancy is equally damaging because the baby has no opportunity to practice adaptability; a move to a new home will give him nightmares. In either case, the child is launched toward the vivid wretchedness of a neurosis: anxiety is part of every neurotic personality and may even be the foundation of them all.

Psychology only recently discovered anxiety. Even thirty years ago, only a few thoughtful men had even noticed it. Among these were Sigmund Freud and Sören Kierkegaard— and the latter's translators term the state "dread," rather than anxiety. Today anxiety dominates psychology and psychiatry periodicals and conferences, permeates research of human motivation, North American women, alcoholism, delinquency, homosexuality, addiction, heart disease, nervous breakdowns, tension and stress. Anxiety has come to be the universal word, it turns up in every diagnosis. If mental health is "deeply felt happiness," as Dr. Dallas Pratt claims, then mental illness is deeply felt anxiety.

Dr. Raymond B. Cattell, research professor of psychology at the University of Illinois, in 1964 described anxiety as "a lack of confidence, a sense of guilt and worthlessness, a dependency, a readiness to become fatigued, irritable and discouraged, an uncertainty about oneself and a suspicion of others, and a general tenseness."

The tardy recognition of the importance of anxiety is due to the centuries-old tendency to call it fear whenever it showed itself and depression whenever it didn't. Fear is hard-edged and can name its real enemy, while anxiety is diffuse and plumps up fake monsters.

The study of anxiety was given great impetus in North America when psychologists seized on the notion that anxiety is directly responsible for drive. Since nothing fascinates this culture so much as ambition and hustle, all hands fell to and attempted to distill anxiety in some pure state that could be fed to sluggish dreamers. The first notable achievement was the discovery that man can readily induce a breakdown in animals. A tiny white mouse, separated from its kind in a solid-walled cage, becomes insane in two weeks. Rats, punished when they jumped and punished when they didn't jump, rapidly became frantic. Sheep and goats, broken down when young by monotony, regular shocks ten seconds apart and darkness, remained neurotic all their lives. A man at Cornell University spent twenty-two years of his life causing breakdowns in animals. His experiments and those of hundreds of cohorts flowed from an accidental discovery in Pavlov's laboratory, where one of the most intelligent dogs had a nervous breakdown a few days after a freak flood nearly drowned the animal. Until then, it had been widely believed that only humans had enough imagination to become mentally ill.

Most experimenters have too much respect for the magic beanstalk propensity of anxiety ever to instill a seed of it in a person, so they have contented themselves with measuring the quotas of anxiety already existing within subjects, usually university students, and their behavior under anxiety-provoking situations.

The results have been interesting, though they have failed to illuminate the nature of anxiety. At Northwestern University, psychologist Janet A. Taylor developed a method of measuring anxiety in individuals. Called the Taylor Anxiety Scale (TAS), it consisted of a list of two hundred and seventy-five statements, fifty of which had been found to be fairly certain clues to anxiety. These included: I am often sick to my stomach; I worry quite a bit over possible troubles; I wish I could be as happy as others; life is often a strain for me; I certainly feel useless at times; I feel hungry almost all the time; I have nightmares every few nights; I am easily embarrassed; I have been afraid of things or people that I know could not hurt me.

With TAS and other measuring devices, researchers have discovered that highly anxious people are impelled to do well in situations which require rote learning but fall apart as soon as competition or the need for flexibility are introduced.

Studies of anxiety in children have demonstrated, as many psychologists anticipated, that those free of inordinate anxiety come from homes where the family is relaxed and friendly and the children both adored and disciplined. Overpunished and underadmired children test highest in anxiety.

The direct result of almost every unpleasant family relationship is an increased load of anxiety on the children. Dr. Karen Horney, psychoanalyst-writer, once observed, "A wide range of adverse factors in the environment can produce this insecurity in a child: direct or indirect domination, indifference, erratic behavior, lack of respect for the child's individual needs, lack of real guidance, disparaging attitude, too much admiration or the absence of it, lack of reliable warmth, having to take sides in parental disagreements, too much or too little responsibility, over-protection, isolation from other children, injustice, discrimination, unkept promises, hostile atmosphere . . ."

The normal development of every child already contains dozens of heightened anxiety crises: starting school, a new baby in the home, academic and athletic challenges, illnesses and—most of all—adolescence and its consequent sexuality. A child already driven to the edge of his resources by his poor relationship at home cannot function effectively against these added pressures. Instead of going through them and gaining a measure of wisdom and maturity, he is apt to evade by some technique that seems to work, such as being a bully or a baby. The hurdle that overanxious children are least likely to navigate is puberty and failure in this area may consign them to lifelong childishness. "It is impossible for anyone to mature fully without coming to grips with the sex drive," psychoanalyst Harry Stack Sullivan insists. Anxiety, he wrote, prevents the development of genuine love.

The relationship between anxiety and sex is a curious one. Since anxious people are always lonely as well, the sex act with its reciprocal gifts can be a powerful antidote and rest their souls—but anxiety most cruelly inhibits sex, making it self-conscious and cold. As a result, taut neurotics who most need the priceless peacefulness of a well-consummated sex act are the least likely people in the world to achieve it.

The most accepted theory about anxiety is that it derives from the fear of separation. For this reason babies feel it most acutely when apart from their mothers and adults when confronted with something outside their experience. Since anxiety is so close to fear, it results in certain preparations within the body to meet what the mind has conceived as dangerous. Unhappily, the danger that anxiety dreads is within, and cannot be confronted. The overreadied body eventually wears out—as Antisthenes said, "devoured by its own disposition as iron is by rust."

Doctors are beginning to suspect that anxiety underlies all physical illness to the same extent as it does emotional frailty. It is known to be a strong factor in hyperthyroidism, heart disease, epilepsy, peptic ulcer, hypertension, frequency of urination, excessive appetite or no appetite, asthma, diarrhea, profuse sweating, pallor and flushing, feelings of panic, tension, irritability, inability to concentrate, nausea, fatigue, sleeplessness, restlessness, aching muscles. Dr. Robert B. Malmo of McGill University once reported that pains in the leg may be associated with unconscious anxiety about sex and pains in the arms and shoulders with unconscious hostility.

Migraine headaches are suspected to be the result of days or weeks of steadily increasing anxiety and blocked anger. Dr. Harold G. Wolff, assistant professor of neurology and psychiatry at Cornell University, in 1950 told the Mooseheart Symposium on Feelings and Emotions that migraines go together with overalertness, tension, perfectionism, delayed decisions and the relentless search for approval. To prevent these disorders, more knowledge concerning the origin of these patterns in childhood is necessary, he stated, adding, "The pursuit of these matters is a prime medical responsibility of our day." It remains so today.

Impressive as the physical damage of anxiety is proven to be, its destruction of personality is even graver. Dr. Karen Horney likens the anxious neurotic to a person who spends his entire life in a trench under constant shellfire. The trench can be made quite comfortable but the view from it is weird, full of imagined dangers and horror. The embattled individual perfects the survival technique that worked best for him as a child. Dr. Horney claims that anxious people select one of three main methods: *moving toward people*, which means they become endearing, overappreciative, oversolicitous, and simultaneously have a gluttonous need for praise and a hysterical reaction to criticism; *moving against people*, which results in a need to control others and in emotional inhibitions, looking for the advantage to themselves in all relationships; and *moving away from people*, the numb, uncertain, secretive hiders, who feel safe only when the world keeps its distance.

Neurotics construct these unreal personalities on a false premise: that they are threatened from without. From this wrong start, strange weeds flourish. In order to feel competent against the treachery he believes he sees, the person must build up a sense of power and rightness within himself. He is required to give reverence to this phony, defend it violently and try to believe it. The effort is so exhausting and futile that eventually he loses interest in living and merely goes through the motions. He no longer has the capacity, as Dr. Horney says, "to wish for anything wholeheartedly."

Along the way, his anxiety will attach itself most strongly to circumstances that upset him most as a young child. A tense mother and father are as contagious as Typhoid Mary and if they exhibit hand-wringing when their toddlers are ill or injured there is a likelihood that those children will always be uneasy about ill health and accidents, and will be oversensitive to pain or impairment. Dr. Judson S. Brown, professor of psychology at the State University of Iowa, told the first Nebraska Symposium on Motivation in 1953 that anxiety about money was conditioned by parents who constantly discussed financial problems in a worried manner. The child of such parents may grow up to be an anxious adult, obsessed with the idea that material success is what he needs in order to feel at peace. He can never get enough money to achieve his goal, however, because his basic anxiety isn't to be soothed with any palliative except maturity.

Similarly, a child who was punished repeatedly for getting his clothes dirty will become an adult who is uncomfortable when taking part in outdoor games or hikes. A child over-cautioned about the hazards of being venturesome is apt to be hampered by his distrust of novelty for the rest of his days. A child whose parents don't love one another but are too emotionally restrained to argue will be puzzled and worried and—according to psychoanalyst Erich Fromm—may withdraw into daydreams and prefer a tone of masochism in his life because palpable violence relieves the anxiety he feels in the presence of concealed rage. Stiff and demanding mothers, who won't permit their children to lose their tempers and demand only "goodness" from them, can produce children who live in anxiety and agitation, with a sense of something hanging over their heads.

Paul Tillich, the brilliant and controversial theologian, lists three forms of anxiety: the anxiety of death, the anxiety of meaninglessness and the anxiety of guilt and condemnation. The middle one, he says, is the most characteristic of this age. In a desolate search for the meaning of their lives, people turn hopefully to religion. Dr. Tillich warns, "A spiritual center cannot be produced intentionally, and the attempt to produce it only produces deeper anxiety."

The anxiety about death is most prominent in people who haven't really lived their lives or used their capacities; they exist, propelled along by routine, in the inert hope that vitality will happen to them, and the dread that death will arrive first. The anxiety of meaninglessness is man's recognition of the cosmic absurdity of his self-importance. The anxiety of condemnation is the bitter gift of a cold conscience which punishes everything but pain.

Erich Fromm calls this the marketing culture, a period of human history when commerce and competition and change dominate. It tends to increase the feelings of loneliness and insignificance in individuals. "In fact," Dr. Fromm writes, "the more his primary ties to family, state, church, tradition, social order are broken—without sufficient development of self-strength—the more he is exposed to the painful sense of isolation and helplessness which always underlies the escape from freedom."

Only a few people have the wit and determination to develop self-strength. In one way and another, most duck the dull, hard work of facing themselves. Sometimes they evade their anxiety by becoming ill. Dr. Jean Davey, physician in chief of Women's College Hospital in Toronto, noted in a speech in 1962 that such people are then much sicker than the sick person who has learned to cope with life. Some anxious people hope to convert their diffuse panic into a real fear, which is much easier to endure, and therefore court danger.

Others perform temporary frontal lobotomies on themselves, by getting drunk, taking sedation, barbiturates or tranquilizers, gorging themselves with food or promiscuity. All these serve to wipe out, for a time, awareness of being alone, which is the foundation of anxiety.

Human communication also eases anxiety, which is why a man in a strange city will need to establish a friendly relationship with a bartender. In order to diminish anxiety, people look for common interests and common outlooks with others and accordingly cannot help but despise and fear a differing opinion or custom. Divergence increases anxiety; sameness is assuring.

Quite frequently, adults believe themselves to be healed of acute anxiety. They endured severe attacks of it in their teens and early in their marriages and careers, but the beast seems to be dead. It is therefore devastating to find that some innocent situation can provoke a full attack of excruciating anxiety all over again. A woman who was certain she had licked her fear of falling moved to a new home that she had to reach by crossing a bridge over a ravine; she discovered she could not walk on it. A man who had been uncomfortable as a child at being left alone in the house was nauseated and choked with anxiety when some friends left him by himself in a hunting lodge for a few hours. It is humiliating to be so readily returned to childishness.

Nevertheless, it is only in their late thirties and forties that people who have been anxious since their infancies can finally face the realization that the source of anxiety is within themselves. All other external explanations have to be attempted before most people can arrive at this bleak truth.

The first task is the acceptance of aloneness, isolation, separateness, which is the lot of all human beings. Carl G. Jung writes, "Neither family, nor society, nor position can save him from it, nor the most successful adaptation to actual surroundings, nor yet the most frictionless fitting in with them. The development of personality is a favor that must be paid for dearly."

The payment exacted for a victory over anxiety generally is an extra dose of anxiety. No man can defeat anxiety until he endures the full amount of it contained by himself. He must find what makes him anxious, do it and bear it. His clues that he is on the right track are his own distress and the thudding of his heart and the quickening of his speech. There is the trepidation of trying a new method, the lurking fear that the mind may be overbalanced by the attempt and the darting anxiety: it is almost impossible, but it is the only way.

Dr. Karen Horney has observed that the first and best prize that such warriors can win is the discovery that the real self is strong and even more capable than the phony one. This sense of genuine strength has the effect of relaxing the need for vigilance and suspicion and eventually a sense of oneness with the world begins to flower. Out of the facing of isolation comes the ending of it.

There is also an ending to the need to fight, manipulate, avoid or seduce everyone, Dr. Horney continues. Self-contempt disappears, along with the tolerance of abuse and the seeking of power. It is possible to be wholehearted, make decisions, take consequences, respect others, be spontaneous and without pretense.

Reality therapy, the newest tool of psychiatry, clinically imposes courage on the anxious. A woman described by Dr. H. J. Eysenck, professor of psychology at Maudsley Hospital in London, was afraid to go out alone. She was taken on long walks and rides with an attendant and then heavily tranquilized and sent on short trips by herself. Gradually the trips were lengthened and the tranquilizers weakened until she was able to walk long distances by herself and without medication. Similarly, people with special phobias were requested to envision the situation that made them most nervous and while they held this in their minds they were almost hypnotized into relaxing. Children with great fears were exposed to the objects of their anxiety and simultaneously were fed candy and talked to lovingly.

One psychiatrist, Dr. Leo Rangell, made the not facetious comment to the American Psychiatric Association in 1954 that anxious people can perhaps make a decision each morning not to be apprehensive that day. He noted that two of his patients reported that they were free of anxiety during the first few moments after they wakened in the morning, after which they "remembered" and anxiety flooded on them. "Perhaps this is the crucial moment in determining which agencies or principles are to gain ascendency in mental life for the day," he said. He told the story of a 102-year-old man who explained his secret for longevity: "Every morning when I get up I can either feel good or bad for the day. I decide, 'Oh, what the hell,' and I decide to feel good. That's how I live so long."

Walter Lippmann's advice to the anxious has the same beauty of simplicity: Know, he says, that everything changes and everything comes to an end. "An adult has to break his attachment to persons and things," he wrote in A *Preface to Morals.* "He must learn to hold on to things which do not slip away and change, to hold on to things not by grasping them but by understanding them and remembering them. Then he is wholly an adult."

To be wholly an adult is to join the brotherhood of man, an elite group with some notable peculiarities: capacity for trust, ability to love and freedom from anxiety.

CHAPTER TWELVE

Anyone Can Mature

No researcher can weave through the thickness of conflicting experiments, declarations and speculations about the human emotions without finding a scarlet thread that so matches personality and individual experience that it belongs to the finder.

In this book the discovery has been that any adult can deliberately change his character—by acts of will and wisdom, rearrange his own stars and regenerate himself.

A prominent trend in modern psychology is the cynical manipulation of emotions, by poking at the brain with an electric current or plying the bloodstream with chemicals to produce an á-la-carte order of any emotion the scientist desires. It is true that the mood drugs in particular have become vital tools of psychiatry, useful to tide over the very ill. But they have transient benefits that vanish when the treatment stops. For lasting support, man must still rely on his inner resources.

Those who worry a good deal, or are often in a vengeful mood, or are endlessly depressed must bring about their own permanent chemical change and stimulate their brains themselves. The results are less spectacular, being tedious slow, but they last a lifetime.

Psychologists now are revaluating the importance of early environment, for fifty years the inflexible rule to explain almost all adult behavior. It has become necessary to account somehow for the thundering herd of exceptions. Some specialists, notably Harvard's esteemed Gordon W. Allport, have come to believe that a sour childhood makes maturing a lot tougher but not, as was formerly presumed, impossible. An ideal infancy, fortified by tenderness and independence, makes it a cinch for a child to develop his capacity to work, love and enjoy—but apparently it isn't the only ticket of admission to maturity.

The wonder of the world, the spirit of man, keeps humans trying and hoping despite the vilest of situations. From time to time, if fate co-operates, moods of receptiveness will coincide with the advice of a wise man, or the lesson of a failure, or the offering of friendship. It results in a spurt of emotional growth that the experts could never have predicted.

"Man has the capacity, as well as the desire, to develop his potentialities and become a decent human being," psychoanalyst Karen Horney has written. "Man can change and go on changing as long as he lives."

It's a process that most psychologists are only beginning to admit is possible, and none can fully explain. People who mature themselves "have so much to teach us that sometimes they seem almost like a different breed of human beings," commented the eminent Brandeis University psychologist, Dr. Abraham H. Maslow.

While European psychologists have long been appreciating the human capacity for self-maturing, most North American psychologists have been strongly influenced by Sigmund Freud's concept that lifelong character is determined before the age of three. Freud believed that later events may modify a man's personality slightly, but no profound change was possible.

It seemed a sound enough view for most of the past half century. Deeply neurotic or mentally ill adults almost invariably have been shown to be the products of a childhood that lacked maternal love and stability. Affection-deprived babies, particularly those reared in institutions, were found in the 1940s to be mutilated by distrust, anger and depression. Disturbed children (or "detached" children as some social workers prefer to call them) generally have a weak or cruel or absent father and a mother who inherently dislikes them.

All this fitted Freud's theory of the permanence of early damage perfectly. Then, a few years ago, scientists began to seek out a new subject for research, one who had never appealed for their help: the healthy, flourishing adult. They found, as anticipated, that productive and happy men and women often had been raised in productive, happy homes, where the parents loved them enough to discipline them, grant them autonomy and instill confidence.

But just as often, they found stable, cheerful, resourceful adults who had endured wretched childhoods which, according to all the known rules, should have incapacitated them for normal living. Neglected, abused, pampered or pushed as toddlers, they somehow gathered enough sense and steadiness to confound the experts and mature themselves.

Indeed, for many people maturity is possible only after an emotional or mental breakdown, when they have experienced such horror that the new personality that they construct on the ruins of their inadequacies is built only of true parts that are impervious to stress. The late Albert Camus, the French writer-philosopher, once reflected, "In order to become aware of our eternity, we need to be forced into our last bastion."

The study of the far reaches of human emotional possibilities is so difficult and tortuous because of its newness, observed Dr. Maslow. "It has involved for me the continuous destruction of cherished axioms, the perpetual coping with seeming paradoxes, contradictions and vagueness and the occasional collapse around my ears of long established, firmly believed in and seemingly unassailable laws of psychology."

Dr. Maslow began studying mature people in 1940 and found them so inconsistent and out of kilter with the doctrines he had always trusted that he didn't begin to publish his findings until ten years later. Since mature people are no longer interested in maintaining a set personality pattern, they fluctuate blissfully and utterly exasperate scientists who lack the wit to be flexible.

"At high levels of human maturation, many dichotomies, polarities and conflicts are fused and resolved," Dr. Maslow noted. "Self-actualizing people are simultaneously selfish and unselfish, rational and irrational. They tolerate their own inconsistencies and contradictions and see a kind of wisdom in conflicts . . ." They have some qualities in common: moral standards, for instance, are set by themselves rather than society and their dominant quality is respect for life; their general tone is moderate, detached, comfortable, sensible, unpretentious. Many are former radicals who have come to appreciate subtlety. A great many passed through a long period of depression, when they thought themselves worthless and life futile.

Little is yet charted in this new land of the self-realized. One conjecture is that the process probably takes place somewhat later than physical maturing. Dr. Maslow found no one mature who was younger than thirty-five.

The twenties seem to be an extension of adolescence at best, and more often of childhood. The favorite adult subjects for researches are college students, since they are plentiful and handy, but they rarely pick up immutable truths about maturity from this age group. People in their twenties have multi-personalities, none of which may even come close to resembling their own essence. Young people mutter to themselves over old grudges, bridle readily at criticism, demand love from all their contacts and are disgusted with themselves, between streaks of believing themselves infallible.

But during their thirties, many people can find their own heartbeats at last. Their vitality for the first time can be matched by enough experience to give it rewarding direction.

These may be mankind's best growth years in terms of psychological development, comparable in importance with his infancy. Fate may have cheated him of a good start, but he has in his golden years another chance to learn self-acceptance and develop insight.

There is a significant parallel: most of mankind's towering achievements are produced by men in their thirties. Harvey C. Lehman was fascinated with the relationship between age and peak performance and spent twenty years searching history in order to compose hundreds of meticulous graphs. He found that major contributions by men of genius were made while they were between thirty and forty years of age. The list includes mathematicians, physicists, inventors, writers, astronomers, composers, psychologists (starting with Aristotle), artists, founders of religions (including Christ), educators, sculptors, surgeons, actors, philosophers and explorers.

The thirties are the years when a man's inner fire burns at its lifelong best. If he is going to make it, he becomes master of himself in those years or the early ones of his forties. He is independent of both the need to be mothered and the compulsion to dominate. He sees the world as it really is, and not as it must be in order to preserve his sanity.

There are traces of this secret force for identity in the perversity which causes a baby to run gleefully away from outstretched arms or wriggle imperiously off a comfortable lap. These are the earliest symptoms of man's insistence on being separate, special, his own self. This innate resistance to encirclement, so pronounced in well-loved children, may be the same mysterious and divine spirit that protects some children who are exposed to such psychic scurvies as rejection, or indifference, or brutality, or overprotection. They deflect some of the harm by the stubbornness of their faith in their own worth.

Some suspect that heredity may influence the strength of this private interior warrior. It may be that spunk is a legacy of generations of men and women who liked and kept their individuality.

The seventeenth century Dutch philosopher, Benedict Spinoza, called this quality *cognatus*, the tendency of the person to persist, though the furies howl, in marching to his own drum. It seems to be the sacred ingredient that truly directs destiny, a compound of courage, resolution and attunement to self. Everyone is born with a lot of it; some people never touch their supply at all.

The drama of existence is the struggle between this life-loving heroic force and the discouragements, afflictions and fearfulness of normal living. Putting in the years, many dully wait for their unhappiness to go away, in torpid expectation of magic. They dream of a challenge to test themselves against, and fancy that they will triumph—but are unaware that the war they envision is already in progress and all the battles are small incidents, conversations, thoughtful acts, trivialities of human exchange.

Others, the scrappers, simply buckle down and mature themselves. No man's method is of much use to anyone else, since every human act is unique and unrepeatable, but the self-matured have left a few blazes.

One is the general tilt they decided to give themselves toward a more loving and useful life. Carl Jung defined personality as the state toward which a man is growing: not the transient thing he is, but what he is planning to make of himself. Socrates said, "The important thing is to keep moving in the right."

Tenacity is vital, because the early stages of self-maturing are as failure-prone as the early stages of walking. There are no discernible victories with the sound of trumpets and the relatives agog, but all failures are disconcertingly public. The process is one of penetrating Chinese boxes; every advancement is innately desolating because a different box is revealed, one requiring a brand new and unimaginable key. Eventually the irritations and frustrations give way; there is a silent sensation of fragile unfolding and a belief in self begins. The rest is sheer confirmation.

The skirmishes of self-development are dreary, boring and

lonely. They involve a review of grievances from a new point of view—someone else's—and the burial of same. They require privacy, the scarcest commodity in the twentieth century, in order to sort the gains and losses. There must be a deepening of some friendships by giving genuine compassion instead of small talk and an abandoning of those which are enduringly superficial and exhausting. Energy-wasters must be eliminated: clubs, social events, needless appointments, errands, vacuous conversations, status hobbies. The heart of life, family, good friendships, work and valuable contributions must be done full out, to the best of ability. Most guilt is illusion and must be scotched; the past is over and the present is in more capable hands. There must be a willingness to risk ridicule in the interest of ethics. The brain must become vivid enough to record more color, more scent, more music.

It is a tactic of modern psychiatry to treat the symptoms and let the disease fend for itself. Called reality therapy, it has some astounding results. Alcoholics Anonymous, for instance, is one of the most successful examples of reality therapy. A communion of persons, interlocked in honesty and understanding, effects mutual healing. For another example, a taut television performer betrayed her inner hysteria by speaking in a shrill high-pitched voice. She sought a doctor, hoping for a bottle of tranquilizers. "Tone your voice down," he told her. "That's all that is the matter." She did it, and the one successful effort at control led to nearly total composure.

An actor, suffering from agonizing ulcers, cured them by becoming an ardent Jungist and believing in human spaciousness. The wife of an executive, promoted to a job that required him to travel a great deal, began to have such intense headaches that the pain made her moan. Neurological tests revealed no physical cause so she sat down with herself and figured it out: she hated her husband's job and wanted him home. Her headaches vanished and, as an offering to the gods, she put some of her spare time into helping retarded children.

A young man who had hoped to be a concert pianist took a civil service job to tide him over the first years of a marriage. Children arrived and he found himself advancing in his occupation. One morning he discovered that an ulcer had perforated his stomach wall. During his convalescence, he considered himself: he could not support his family without the civil service job, and his family was more important to him than the unlikely possibility of a concert career. To his own astonishment, the mere recognition of his underlying problem relieved his ulcer condition.

Doctors often instruct patients who are highly anxious because their lives seem meaningless, "Don't worry so much." They also tell chronic coughers to stop coughing and people with some types of knee injury to stop limping. The principle is the same: coughing irritates membranes and increases coughing, limping keeps the knee sore and a state of worry is a worry in itself.

Such advice, sympathetically intended and medically sound, has the immediate effect of increasing pain. It hurts to walk staunchly on a wrenched knee, and containing a cough gives one the sensation of being throttled. It is even more agonizing to try to switch desperate thoughts. Some people hope to accomplish it by smiling more, but the effect is one of a grotesque mask and the eyes that stare out are those of a convict with a life sentence. Others try to overwhelm their inner sickness with fervent work, or socializing, or travel and other novelties; the sickness remains underwhelmed.

Only a few are able to follow what seems like inane advice. They stand off from themselves, as far as their skill permits, and make a hard-edged assessment. Something is going wrong: too much stress (where?), distractions that are inane, too much loneliness, too little usefulness. They reorganize their timetables and switch the emphasis around so that effort will be rewarded with humanity's first prize, a sense of worth. Sometimes the change is made in a musing minute, outside the doctor's office; sometimes it takes ten years. Either way, it's growth and divine.

What psychoanalyst Erich Fromm calls the North American "marketing orientation" leads some people to decide that maturity is the knack of having a successful personality. In endeavoring to rid themselves of self-hatred they grin more, criticize less, applaud insanely and join everything. Their dismay, when this fails to make them happy, is the final demoralizing blow. Behind the grind of joviality, they scream silently for help—and no one hears.

Human beings are too complicated to advance by moving in only one direction. Every adult carries with him a jostling assortment of more or less primitive emotions, rage, hate and fear, which civilizing can render reasonable but never remove. Wiping them off surface personality is a venture into suicide. Instead of arguments, the man or woman will have cardiac failure; instead of showing hatred, an ulcer will develop; instead of admitting illogical fear, it is easier to be a bigot.

Self-maturing only partially involves warmer, kinder treatment of one's fellow men. It is also imperative to become nastier—to lose one's temper gloriously in an appropriate situation, to detest loudly unequal laws, tyrants and all forms of execution, to snarl without concern for dignity at exploitation and falseness.

The secret of maturity isn't the smothering of socially unpleasant emotions. The heart of the matter is the development of self-acceptance. Adults who were blessed with loving, vigorous parents have enough of this to mature without much struggle, but most people have to grow their own self-respect. It's a clairvoyant plant, not in the least impressed by popularity or wealth or achievement. It derives its bloom from the worthiness of an individual's existence: his honesty with himself, his integrity about his responsibilities, his decency toward all forms of life.

"It is always better to learn to bear with ourselves rather than to wage war against ourselves," declared Carl Jung. "To forswear hypocrisy and to adopt an attitude of tolerance toward oneself can only have good results for the just estimation of one's neighbor, since men are all too prone to transfer to their fellow men the injustice and violence that they do their own natures. He who feels in a bad way with himself and wishes to improve . . . must take counsel with himself. For unless a man changes inwardly as well, external changes in the situation are either unimportant or even harmful."

Dr. Maslow states, "Every person is, in part, his own project and makes himself."

A man who has realized himself, piercing through his own phoniness to find his own viable core, is a celestial unity. He is a stranger to anxiety; his anger is rare and spends itself as entirely as a child's; his moods of depression are piquant rather than pulverizing; he is highly sociable and also is deeply satisfied by being solitary; the battle of the sexes is over for him, since gender doesn't seem threatening. He looks marvelous, bright-eyed, relaxed and warm-skinned. His allegiance is total, to all of life. Best of all, he loves.

In *World* magazine, Geoffrey Leytham wrote, "Few people are mentally sick and few people mentally well. The majority are just not hungry, their appetite for life has become dulled. It is as if the delights of childhood had been swamped by the cares of the adult. In the mature person, on the other hand, the wonderment and excitement of a child are combined with the experience and wisdom of an adult. The healthy person is a craftsman in the art of living."

"As you value men's lives," comments novelist Bernard Malamud, "yours receives value. Any act of good is a diminution of evil in the world."

The awareness of the latent power for self-reformation within everyone has led to some startling new approaches to the problem of juvenile delinquency. One of the pioneers is a California detention school psychiatrist, Dr. William Glasser. He declares, "The more delinquent children are convinced by tradition therapy that they are disturbed and have good reason to be so, the worse they will act in and out of custody."

He therefore takes no history, is not interested in the background that produced the errant behavior. He informs the delinquent flatly that he is not in custody because he is an emotional problem (which the boy has been comforting himself with) but because he has broken the law.

"We never excuse any action, past or present, directly or indirectly, by asking why or seeking the answer in the unconscious," Dr. Glasser explains. "No matter how severe the personality disorder, we maintain that removed from the atmosphere where excuses are accepted the boy has adequate standards. We may admit he was mistreated, but we emphasize . . . that he can't excuse his behavior because someone has rejected him."

The same technique of demanding sanity is being tested in at least one mental hospital as well. Dr. G. L. Harrington in Los Angeles treats all his patients with this reality therapy and reports it is highly successful. The technique is spreading like a fire in the wind. One psychiatrist with a woman patient who seemed completely out of control at home, where she had dish-breaking tantrums and hours-long bouts of tears, sent her to visit relatives who didn't know she was ill. For the two weeks she was away, the woman was forced to seem normal. She helped with the baking, chatted with callers, sat calmly in the garden. The progress she made, the doctor decided, could not have been equaled by three months of hospitalization.

Inside every depressed, anxious and angry adult there apparently is a reasonable, mellow and friendly personality struggling to emerge. "We take the approach," a Toronto psychiatric social worker related, "that each person has the ability within him or herself to handle things." Dr. Glasser has yet to meet a juvenile offender who lacked adequate standards. He summons out coherent behavior by insisting on it, while lavishly praising every success. This is the actual condition for maturing: interior and exterior demand for it, plus plenty of support.

Dr. Fromm, whose philosophy has a vast following, addressed a gathering in a Toronto synagogue in 1963 and was asked plaintively from the floor for a "practical solution" to the problems of living. He replied instantly, "Concentration, for a half hour every day, twice a day if possible."

The audience sighed in disappointment. "I'm serious," Dr. Fromm declared. "You have to stop in order to be able to change direction. Quietness, the experience of stillness, is an important requirement for mental health. Stop the mental and physical rush and you will stop being a stranger to yourself."

It's an answer with little appeal to those who like forceful directions with their do-it-yourself kits, but most authorities agree with Dr. Fromm that periods of tranquillity are vital for emotional growth. Harried, frazzled, tired men and women lose ground in their attempts to mature. The hard task of taking stock of a lifetime's debris of opinions requires solitude and a rested mind. Major matters, such as recognizing the self-interest and lack of love in a proprietary relationship, can't be resolved in the haphazard drift of undercurrent thought that streams beneath business discussions, waiting for buses, ironing blouses.

Emotions, it seems, mature by an emotional process. They need quietness in order to consolidate the gains made during the hustle and monotony of ordinary living, and they also need sociability, to keep them limber. Curiously, intellect is of very little help in psychological development. Psychologists and psychiatrists have been known to botch their private lives miserably and to produce distraught children. The emotions appear to be baffled by book knowledge; they learn only what they already knew. The wordless mind gathers impressions from intuition and experience and when these are ready, and not a day sooner, words on a page make glorious sense. Otherwise textbooks, philosophies, essays and advice are all purest Sanskrit.

But nature has a bonus, a free one, that many regard as the world's greatest aid to maturity. Dr. Maslow terms this gift a "peak experience" and says everyone gets two or three in a lifetime. As maturity progresses, peak experiences become more frequent.

Peak experiences are raptures: they are suspended outside of time, so there is no awareness of the passing minutes or hours; there is a feeling of fusion with earth, heaven and all life; objects have a clarity and freshness never noticed before and passing faces are beautiful with dignity. People and circumstances observed during peak experiences don't alert the ego, which has no need to use them for gain. Concentration is stunningly acute but effortless. There is no limit to tolerance and pity; human misdeeds don't seem shameful or cruel, but only sad. When the peak experience gently evaporates, the person is left dazed, thrilled and exalted. The sensation has been so transcending that to descibe it afterwards seems coarse and unappreciative.

"Peak experiences in some cases remove neurotic symptoms forever," Dr. Maslow says. In any case, they provide the individual with a knowledge of perfection, against which he is uniquely able to define all the lesser states more common to existence. Having discovered the bliss of total coherence, he is heartened about the possibilities of living. Peak experiences grace the condition of man with palpable happiness, infusing courage and confidence.

Sometimes peak experiences arise from the obvious, such as a declaration of mutual love, or a superbly timed kindness, or news that a person whose life was in jeopardy is beginning to recover. Sometimes sparkling weather produces the experience in someone who has time to idle in the sunlight. Many people feel luminous when confronted by natural splendor, such as mountains or the sea or a storm. One woman had an evanescent experience on a vile, rainy day in November: she drew the drapes, lit a fire of pine logs, prepared a pot of tea and suddenly felt light and loving. A man, distracted by the needs of a business matter, looked up from lighting a cigarette to read sympathy on the face of his four-year-old daughter and melted inside. Sometimes a decision, bravely taken and intrinsically right, results in a glory of mood; when a man is most moral, he is functioning at the height of his civilized power and this in itself is ecstatic.

Mature people may confuse a psychologist with their unrelated behavior, but they possess such a high sense of integration that it doesn't trouble them in the least. They have crossed the stoney ground of guilty carefulness and repression; in learning about themselves, they uncovered a multitude of idiosyncrasies and all of them seem unimportant. The aliveness that courses through them won't be perverted by calcifying personality into an artful mold. Knowing themselves to be essentially loving, they can trust their reflexes.

Confucius mused about his old age, when he "could follow what my heart desired, without transgressing what was right."

Mature people can endure failure and mistakes in themselves and others because they have grasped the point that perfection is inhuman. Occasionally they solve a problem by behaving like full-fledged neurotics.

Despite their flare for self-selected and spontaneous conduct, mature people generally are unspectacular to know. They conform to the sensible rules of society, observe laws, eschew fads and extremes. Mostly they are calm and affable, gregarious and hospitable, easy to like and believe. They appreciate, and they don't strain.

They have found the truth in Carl Jung's statement that "The greatest and most important problems of life are all fundamentally insoluble . . . They can never be solved, but only outgrown."

"I don't spend precious time any more damning myself," wrote Mackey Brown in a magazine article celebrating the maturity she achieved in her forties. "I will never be beautiful, rich or café society, but I have planted forget-me-nots, nursed a baby, seen the sun rise and stars fall, lain with my love . . . And now I have reached the age of self-discovery."

The age of self-discovery bears with it a sense of permeating awe that can only be described as religion. It's a gift that can't be commanded by determinedly attending church or temple, being attentive to sermons, mulling over the fine print in the Bible. It comes sweetly, of its own accord, when the person grows wise enough to see the grandeur in every living thing. The theologian Paul Tillich calls this highest form of worship, "the God above God."

Once they are aboard, the mature must honor their debt to put down as many ladders as possible for other swimmers. No one who is hungry, cold, friendless and without shelter can have a vision beyond his own grinding needs. In order to unfold their true natures, human beings must be free of gross indignities.

Currently determinists among psychologists are claiming that all human behavior is a response that can be controlled artificially. They say that no human act is truly spontaneous; personality is a jerky dance of puppets. They demonstrate their theory by manipulating emotions. They sink electrodes into the pudding of the brain and tickle it into producing fear, or anger, or pleasure. They employ drugs that can cause the suicidal to feel elation, the anxious to relax and lions to panic.

"It's all done with electricity and chemicals, which suggests to some that this is all there is to the human personality. The will is a myth, the spirit a conditioned reflex, integrity is a superior balance of hormones. "Learn how to feel joy," Seneca advised, to which determinists today retort, "Learn a good prescription and the route to the pharmacy."

The concept is comparable to a biology student's pronouncement that Winston Churchill is composed of water and ninety-six cents worth of chemicals. As Arthur Koestler commented, "Even the lowly worm, sliced into six pieces, knows better."

The distinguished Roman Catholic intellectual, the Very Reverend M. C. D'Arcy, adds, "there is a last mysterious layer in the self that can never really be touched, an ultimate self."

It's the ultimate self that creates miracles: cripples who walk when it was impossible that they could, dying men who become strong again, people with slight intelligences who teach themselves a difficult skill, loving people who have good reason to hate.

Socrates said: "Wonders are many, and none is more wonderful than man."

....other best selling
NEWCASTLE books
you won't want to miss....